What Every Educator Should Know About Using Google™

Author
Kathryn Martin, M.A.

SHELL EDUCATION

Publishing Credits

Dona Herweck Rice, *Editor-in-Chief*; Robin Erickson, *Production Director*;
Lee Aucoin, *Creative Director*; Timothy J. Bradley, *Illustration Manager*;
Sara Johnson, M.S. Ed., *Senior Editor*; Tracy Edmunds, *Associate Education Editor*;
Juan Chavolla, *Cover Designer*; Corinne Burton, *M.A. Ed., Publisher*

Shell Education

5301 Oceanus Drive
Huntington Beach, CA 92649-1030
http://www.shelleducation.com

ISBN 978-1-4258-0823-5

©2012 Shell Educational Publishing, Inc.

Table of Contents

Search

Foreword

I'm so glad I read this book. Not only did I learn new things—and I thought I was Google-wise already—but I also got a new perspective on how the networking and information management tools in Google can work for site administrators, classroom teachers, and students.

Kathy Martin is the perfect person to write it. She was a star classroom teacher and is now a celebrated site administrator. She weaves the book with examples from her students and from the daily tasks of a principal. She also adds data from the big picture. Did you know, for example, that 7.5 million children under 13 had Facebook accounts? (P.S.: They're not supposed to.)

It is good to have this book out there. It will make my job as a workshop leader easier. Two days ago I was in Canada with a group of smart, wired teachers. If everyone in the room, including myself, had the knowledge in *What Every Educator Should Know About Using Google* it would have given us lots of new ways to work with media-based assignments. I'm sure that's true whether the reader is looking for parent connections, book reports, administrator walk-throughs, or other applications Kathy Martin has thought of. All of them have a place in this book. Her "Tips", "Try It," and "Reflection Questions" laced throughout the book nail the content.

For me, the use of Google Drawing with Interactive White Boards and the Advanced Search tip on searching for materials with rights clearances were fantastic. From the big picture and The Cloud down to the click-and-drag for students, there is material in this publication that will open a new world of usage for Google's familiar—and not so familiar—tools.

Hall Davidson,
Director of Global Learning Initiatives,
Discovery Education

What Is Technology?

People have been writing and drawing since they realized they could inscribe their thoughts on rocks and the walls of caves. They have been organizing data since the Babylonian counting board in 300 B.C., and they have been publishing for mass markets since the invention of the printing press by Gutenberg in 1440. The word *technology* originated from the Greek word *techne*, translated as *art, craft, or skill*. Aristotle defined it as a systematic use of knowledge for intelligent human action. Technology, by either ancient or modern definition, should be seen as "a system of practical knowledge not necessarily reflected in things or hardware" (Saetter 1990, 3).

Throughout history, advances in technology have not changed people's desire to read, write, draw, and organize. Instead, technological advances over the centuries, at an ever-increasing pace, have allowed greater numbers of people to participate in these activities in more efficient, productive, and creative ways. We have always used technology. When teaching my fourth graders about technology, I always start by asking, "What is technology?" They consistently name computers, cell phones, mp3 players, and video games. In fact, my students are always shocked and entertained to hear that the invention of the pencil in 1564 constituted "modern technology" at that time. Early man's first fire reflected an advance in technology, along with domestication of animals, irrigation canals, democracy...the list goes on.

Since I purchased my first desktop computer in the late 1980s (for over $3,000, I might add), there have been many changes. I have been thrilled by the programs and functions designed to make my life easier. Word-processing programs, one of the first applications for productivity, were introduced in the 1970s, but were not readily available to office or home users until the eighties. The first PC word-processing program in 1976 was called *Electric Pencil*. In 1979, the first commercially successful word processing program, *Wordstar,* was released. Then along came Microsoft® and Apple® and the rest is history.

The pace of technological change continues to increase. It was not long ago that cutting-edge technology consisted of filmstrips and overhead projectors. Fifty years from now it will be interesting to see if future generations wonder how educators of the past managed to teach with only streaming video, slide-show software, and high-definition projectors. Technology is moving ahead at an ever-faster pace to help educators and students read, write, draw, and organize in more productive and creative ways.

The Cloud

Do you remember when "walking around with your head in the clouds" was a bad thing? Nowadays, if your head isn't in the clouds at least part of the day, you are behind the times. Our students were born with their heads in the clouds, but many educators today are striving to get their heads in the clouds before the clouds pass them by. Having your head in "The Cloud" today is different than it was only a few years ago.

If you were to ask 50 different people to define "The Cloud," you would probably get 50 different answers. People in different fields use the term "Cloud Computing" in many ways. The National Institute of Standards and Technology provides a concise and specific definition:

"Cloud computing is a model for enabling convenient, on-demand network access to a shared pool of configurable computing resources (e.g., networks, servers, storage, applications, and services) that can be rapidly provisioned and released with minimal management effort or service provider interaction" (2011, 2).

The Cloud enables real-time delivery of products and services over the Internet. For the purpose of this book, working in The Cloud is defined as taking advantage of tools and applications via the Internet, without downloading any software onto a computer.

Everything you need to be productive is available in The Cloud. Cloud services include software, networking, infrastructure, and applications available through the Internet. What this means to you and me is that there is a complex and exciting world of computing out there, and not only is it accessible but, in many cases, it is free! I love free stuff. All teachers love free stuff. That is why my head is in The Cloud daily.

Entire school districts have caught cloud-computing fever. This is because students and educators can access information in The Cloud anywhere, any time, through the Internet. In its quest to save money, the Kentucky Department of Education is looking to The Cloud to bring communication and collaboration to 700,000 students, faculty, and staff statewide. Kentucky expects to save $6.3 million over the next four years by moving to cloud-based computing (eSchoolNews 2010).

The beauty of The Cloud is that it is not only accessible to states, districts, and schools, but individual educators also have the power of The Cloud at their fingertips. There are many clouds, but the largest are Microsoft®, Amazon®, and Google. This book shows you how to take advantage of the tools available in Google's cloud. "Googling in The Cloud" simply means using Google's applications while they are on Google's servers and not your own.

Why Google in The Cloud?

We've all "Googled." Google has become a verb for most people. We use Google's powerful search engine every day. How many times have we Googled content while preparing a lesson? Our students Google during class, in the computer lab, and while they do their homework. But did you know that there is much more to Google than just a search engine? Even more powerful for educators are Google tools. Google tools are web-based applications, usually available for free, that can be accessed from any computer because they live in Google's cloud. All you need is a computer with an Internet connection and you can effectively communicate and collaborate. Google's mission is to organize the world's information and make it universally accessible. Isn't this our mission as educators as well?

Google tools can contribute to positive school reform. As teachers, we constantly look for innovative ways to collaborate with each other and to increase collaboration among our students. With Google Docs, a document can be shared among students and with the teacher as well. If Suki and David are assigned a report on Ancient Rome, they can share a Google document. Suki can be at home working on her portion while David works on the same document at the library. When they share their document with their teacher, the teacher has the power to make comments and track their work while they are writing the report. The teacher does not have to wait until there is a stack of 35 rough drafts sitting on the desk awaiting approval.

Google Presentations allow students to work in groups to create sophisticated presentations. With other presentation software, it is not unusual to see a group of students huddled around one monitor, arguing over what font to use on the slides. When students use Google Presentations, they may create and edit slides from the comfort of their own computers—at school, at home, the library, or even at a coffee shop. When you invite students to use sophisticated tools, they become sophisticated learners.

Google tools can also improve your professional productivity. How many times have you headed home at the end of the day and realized, "I left my rubric on my computer! Do I turn back and get it, or just go home and do it over again? If only I had emailed it to myself..." Sometimes we turn back, many times we create the whole thing over again, and occasionally we have to add it to our to-do list the following day. With Google Docs, the rubric would be waiting in The Cloud to be accessed from a home desktop or laptop. Problem solved!

When it comes to Google, productivity is the name of the game. Why do productivity tools matter? The tools provided by Google are aimed at saving time and meeting needs. In 1998, Google entered the marketplace and became the most successful search engine because it was the best at meeting the needs of users searching for information on the Internet.

The face of the web has changed over the years, and Google aims to keep changing with it. Google published its philosophy in 2005, and it hasn't changed much. Among its ten core principles, the one at the top of the list is, "Focus on the user and all else will follow."

> *Since the beginning, we've focused on providing the best user experience possible. Whether we're designing a new Internet browser or a new tweak to the look of the homepage, we take great care to ensure that they will ultimately serve **you**, rather than our own internal goal or bottom line.*
>
> (Google: Ten Things We Know to Be True)

The very last of Google's ten core principles reads, "Great just isn't good enough."

> We try to anticipate needs not yet articulated by our global audience, and meet them with products and services that set new standards...and we're always looking for new places where we can make a difference. Ultimately, our constant dissatisfaction with the way things are becomes the driving force behind everything we do.
>
> (Google: Ten Things We Know to Be True)

How to Use This Book

Throughout the book, information is highlighted in the following special sections:

- **Try It** sections provide step-by-step, hands-on practice using many of Google's online tools.

- **Tip** sections offer helpful hints and extra information about specific features and procedures.

- **In the Classroom** sections present strategies and advice for using Google tools with students.

- **Reflection Questions** at the end of each chapter enable reflection on what has been learned in the chapter and stimulate thinking about how to apply that learning.

The *Google Search*, *Google Tools*, and *Google Sites* chapters will walk you through how to use these online Google tools. *Google in the Classroom* and *Increasing Your Productivity with Google* suggest numerous ways to put Google to work in your classroom, school site, or district.

You do not need to read the pages in this resource straight through like a traditional book. You are encouraged to turn to the chapter that most appeals to you at the moment, but ideally you will visit the other chapters as well. This is a reference book, written "from the trenches" by an educator for educators. Keep your computer nearby and try everything as you go. Write in the margins. Highlight what works for you. Start with one Google tool and once you are comfortable with it, add another. The end goal is for you and your students to gain full advantage of Google's educational power.

Keep in mind that Google is constantly updating its applications and services. As updates are made, the tools and commands may be different than what is described in this resource.

Chapter 1

Why Google? | Search

Why should we use technology in the classroom? Some teachers hold technology close to their hearts and others are still wondering why they must have any technology in their classrooms at all. What is so different about today's students that we must teach them in new ways?

21st Century Students

What veteran teachers suspected, the research has proved: 21st Century students are different. With different attention spans, higher IQ test scores, and social networks, their sophistication comes earlier—with a different skill set. There is a silver lining: We can teach this 'New Brain' more effectively, more efficiently, more engagingly. We have the technology! Media has evolved and education must evolve to match.

Hall Davidson, Director, Discovery Education Network

The technology-filled environment in which today's students are immersed is both a challenge and an opportunity for educators. Over a decade ago, in *Digital Natives, Digital Immigrants* (2001), Mark Prensky coined the term "Digital Natives" when speaking of today's students. He states, "Today's students—K through college—represent the first generations to grow up with this new technology. They have spent their entire lives surrounded by and using computers, video games, digital music players, video cameras, cell phones, and all the other toys and tools of the digital age. Today's average college grads have spent less than 5,000 hours of their lives reading, but over 10,000 hours playing video games (not to mention 20,000 hours watching TV). Computer games, email, the Internet, cell phones, and instant messaging are integral parts of their lives" (2001, 1). In fact, according to a national survey by the Kaiser Family Foundation (2010), eight to 18-year-olds today devote an average of seven hours and 38 minutes to using digital media in a typical day. That is more than 53 hours a week.

Karen Cator, Director of the Office of Educational Technology, U.S. Department of Education, has devoted her career to improving learning environments for this generation of students. As an advocate for the integration of digital technology in the classroom, she looks at current reality. Digital media is pervasive. Consider the use of Facebook and Twitter during political uprisings, mobile media coverage of natural disasters such as the tsunami and earthquake in Japan in 2011, or Super Bowl ads that embed secret codes inviting viewers to go online and play games (Cator 2011). In my own home, my children got up early every morning during the summer of 2011 to go online and find the secret quill giving them access to J.K. Rowling's *Pottermore*. It is our job as educators to bring this kind of immediacy and creativity into our classrooms.

The challenge for us as educators is to leverage technology to create learning environments and experiences that mirror our students' daily lives as well as what the future holds for them. Our society is highly mobile and globally connected, and Americans today will have more jobs and more careers in their lifetimes than their parents. It was not long ago that people expected to learn most of the information and skills they needed for life and work in the confines of the school. Now, learning does not stop once a student leaves the classroom; it must be lifelong, lifewide, and available on demand (Bransford et al. 2006). Rather than "Digital Natives," Hall Davidson calls the students of this decade the TAMTAN generation: Try (Touch/Tap) As Many Times As Necessary. Today's students tend to poke around until things work. When it comes to technology, they are natural risk takers and problem solvers. As educators, integrating technology into the classroom allows us to swoop in and take advantage of these eager learners. The opportunity to harness interest and engage these children is huge.

Today's students show an excitement and interest in digital opportunities to learn, so technologists globally have created tools that make collaboration and innovation possible for our students. Ferriter and Garry call today's students, born in the early 1990s, "The iGeneration." They describe the iGeneration as students that can be "inspired by technology to ponder, imagine, reflect, analyze, memorize, recite, and create, but **only** after we build a bridge between what they know about new tools and what we know about good teaching" (Ferriter and Garry 2010, 6).

Whether called Digital Natives, the TAMTANers, or the iGeneration, these are our students and now is the time for making technology an integral part of our students' learning.

Transformational Technology

At one time, student engagement with technology was defined by how many students were actually holding a piece of equipment in their hands, typing on a keyboard, or looking at a website. However, simply *using* technology by playing a drill-and-kill math game on the computer is not enough for our 21st century learners. This is not to say that computer games do not have a place in learning and instruction anymore; it is just that we must look beyond these technologies. Students today must be engaged in learning that requires the use of technology for a specific purpose in which thinking and problem-solving are purposefully embedded. We must ask ourselves, "What can students do with technology now that they couldn't do before?" and, "How can technology enhance students' learning experiences and engage them in the learning process?"

There are two common labels for describing student engagement with technology: *transitional* and *transformational*. *Transitional* engagement means that students are simply using technology to do what they have always done. A student using a presentation application (such as *Microsoft PowerPoint*) instead of giving an oral presentation accompanied by a poster board is an example of transitional engagement. In contrast, *transformational* student engagement means that technology transforms the learning process for students, and often contains some form of higher-order thinking (Fijor 2010). For example, when a student uses Google Docs to compose a research paper, the application essentially acts as a word processor, making this a transitional engagement. However, the collaborative aspect of Google Docs allows the engagement to become transformational. Using this online tool, groups of students can combine their ideas to compose, analyze, and evaluate writing, all within the same document. It is here we see the use of higher-order thinking skills. This engagement is transformational because it allows the process to become collaborative, rather than just an individual experience. The use of technology has now gone from transitional to transformational.

How do we know if students' engagement is transitional or transformational? Technology facilitator Mark Fijor (2010) encourages teachers to ask themselves the following questions when evaluating students' level of engagement with technology:

1. Are students required to use problem-solving or higher-order thinking skills, or does the activity simply require them to recall information?

2. Are the students engaged with technology in a hands-on way, or are they vicariously using the technology through the teacher's use?

18

3. Does the technology serve a purpose that requires students to achieve learning standards, or is it just an additional technology activity?

Transformational technology experiences support and expand good teaching and learning in and out of the classroom. In their book, *Powerful Learning: What We Know About Teaching for Understanding* (2008), Dr. Brigid Barron and Dr. Linda Darling-Hammond remind us that decades of research illustrate the benefits of inquiry-based and cooperative learning to help students develop the knowledge and skills necessary to be successful in a rapidly changing world. Transformational technology tools expand students' capability to work collaboratively and direct their own learning.

Google Tools Are Transformational

Google provides many web-based tools that are truly transformational educational experiences for students at all levels of learning.

- **Google Search** supports and expands inquiry-based learning and requires students to analyze and evaluate as they search for information.

- **Google Documents** provides an avenue of collaboration for students, rather than acting simply as a word processor. With this application, students analyze, evaluate, and create collaboratively during writing and revision through comments, change tracking, and chat.

- **Google Presentation** not only allows students to create a slide show using what they learn, but also allows for real-time collaboration as students narrow their topics, decide on photos for their slides, and create and evaluate their presentation as they go. The backchannel chat feature asks students to analyze and evaluate as they make comments in real time during a presentation.

- **Google Forms** and **Spreadsheets** give students powerful tools to collect and organize data and analyze results, all while working collaboratively.

- **Google Drawing** can be used to create mind maps, brainstorms, outlines, and more. Real-time collaboration is available within this application and students can embed their creations into documents, spreadsheets, presentations, and Web pages.

- **Google Sites** give students an authentic purpose and audience for their writing by allowing them to share their work online with a specific group or with the world.

- **Google+** is a social networking application that allows users to closely control who they share information with. It provides students with opportunities to analyze, create, and evaluate as they communicate with others, design their circles, and choose what to post and to whom.

Google Tools in Bloom's Taxonomy

The collaborative tools available from Google can be used to address learning objectives at multiple levels. On the following page is a chart detailing the Google tools that can be used to create learning experiences for students at each level of Bloom's Taxonomy (Bloom 1956).

Figure 1.1 Bloomin' Google

Creating	Google Sites Google Calendar™ YouTube™ Google Drawings Google Documents
Evaluating	Blogger™ Google Drawings Google Documents Google Presentations Google Groups Google+ Google Earth™
Analyzing	Google Documents Google Groups Google Forms Google Sites Google Drawings Google Spreadsheets Google Earth
Applying	Google Presentations Google Drawings Google Documents Google Spreadsheets Google Sites
Understanding	Google Drawings Google News Google Presentations Google Groups Google Documents Google Advanced Search
Remembering	Google Drawings Google Documents Google Images™ Google+ Google Search

Adapted with permission of Kathy Schrock

©2011. Last updated: 09/07/11. Kathy Schrock. (kathy@kathyschrock.net)
Home page: http://kathyschrock.net/

❓ Reflection Questions

1. How are you currently using technology in your classroom?

2. Are your students' technology experiences in the classroom transitional or transformational?

3. How can you move from giving your students transitional experiences to transformational ones?

4. What technology assistance resources are available to you? Who do you know that can assist you?

Chapter 2

Google Search   Search

I am not sure when Google went from a noun to a verb. It seemed as though it just sort of happened. One day, I went from saying, "I will go to Google.com and search for that topic," to, "Just Google it." In fact, in 2006, the verb "to Google" was added to both the *Oxford English Dictionary* and the *Merriam-Webster Dictionary*. The company, Google, was not thrilled with the addition of "to Google" to the dictionary, as they feared that the meaning of Google would be watered down if it became a general term for using a search engine. The Google permissions website says, "Use the trademark only as an adjective, never as a noun or a verb…." But, despite their reluctance, Google seems to have gone the way of Xerox® and Kleenex® and has become a generic term for searching the Internet.

Why Search?

Current research reveals that if people expect something to remain easily available, they are more likely to remember where they found the information than the information itself—but if they don't think it will be easy to find again, they are more likely to remember the information (Sparrow, et al. 2011). In other words, I may not remember the lyrics to a popular song from high school, but I can certainly remember where I found the information the last time I wanted to know. Or, more practically, my students may not recall the name of the scientist who discovered DNA, but they certainly remember that they "Googled it" before the last test and can "Google it" again the next time they want to know the information. These findings have huge implications for both teaching and learning as we move from traditional memorization to learning experiences that are collaborative, mobile, and student-directed.

> *The advent of the Internet, with sophisticated algorithmic search engines, has made accessing information as easy as lifting a finger. No longer do we have to make costly efforts to find the things we want. We can "Google" the old classmate, find articles online, or look up the actor who was on the tip of our tongue. The results of four studies suggest that when faced with difficult questions, people are primed to think about computers and that when people expect to have future access to information, they have lower rates of recall of the information itself and enhanced recall instead for where to access it. The Internet has become a primary form of external or transactive memory, where information is stored collectively outside ourselves.*

(Sparrow, et al. 2011)

Since research tells us that our students are using the Internet as a form of external memory storage, as educators we must teach our students how to access that information as quickly, accurately, and efficiently as possible. Google search tools provide the power to make that happen.

The Power of Google Search

Most of us have visited Google's home page, typed a word into the search box, and seen three million websites returned. Typically, we click the first link, see what it has to offer, and then return to the results page to click the next link. We keep working our way down the page until we find what we are looking for. It is the same for our students. Many a student will type "Christopher Columbus" into the Google search box and get 40,500,000 results in 0.11 seconds. They often click on the first link, use only the information they find there, and hand in a report on Christopher Columbus the next day. Educators need to show students how to go much further in their search for information. Without high quality instruction, many students will continue to think that Google is a source, not a search engine.

A basic Google search is good, but Google offers many tools and filters that can improve the relevance of search results. These tools can show you things you never knew existed and give you information you didn't even know you needed. Think of the basic Google search as basic arithmetic. When you use Google search tools and filters, you can do calculus. The Google tools listed below will help both you and your students save time and improve the quality of your searches.

- Google SafeSearch
- Google Instant
- Google Instant Preview
- Related Searches
- Find Within Page
- Search by Type of Content
- Google News™
- Google Books™
- Google Images

- Google Videos™
- Dictionary
- Reading Level
- Google Scholar™
- Advanced Search
- Eliminating Unwanted Results
- File Type Search
- Usage Rights Search

Google SafeSearch

Everything and anything is available on the Internet, so it is important to protect students and help them search safely. Google provides a SafeSearch filter which gives parents and teachers tools to help them control what is seen online. SafeSearch is a tool that screens sites and removes explicit content from search results. The SafeSearch default setting is *moderate*, and the moderate setting screens out explicit images, but it might still allow students to stumble across some rather inappropriate websites. To filter out explicit text as well, modify the SafeSearch settings to *strict* by clicking on *Search Settings* in the gear menu at the top right of the Google homepage.

Figure 2.1 Search Settings

Figure 2.2 SafeSearch Filtering

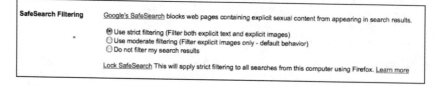

 For added safety, the strict SafeSearch setting can be locked and protected with a password so it cannot be changed. You can tell SafeSearch is on, even from across the room, when you see the colored spheres at the top of a search page.

Figure 2.3 SafeSearch Lock

Search Tools

Google Instant

The first step in a Google search is to type search terms into the search bar. As you type, Google Instant automatically displays popular searches based on what you have typed so far, even before you have completed a word. For example, if "plimou" is typed, Google displays:

Figure 2.4 Google Instant

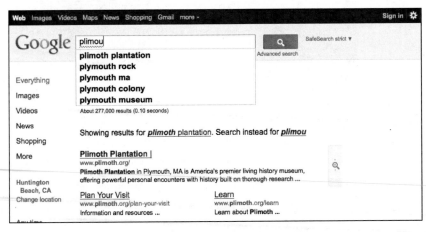

You can continue typing or click any of the displayed options. This tool can be very helpful when you are not sure exactly what you are looking for, and it often gives you related search terms that you never would have come up with on your own. Google Instant also suggests alternate spellings of search terms.

Google Instant Preview

A simple Google search often returns millions of links. How do you know which ones are worth looking at? The Google Instant Preview tool provides a quick idea of what each link has to offer. On a search results page, hover the mouse over the tab to the right of any link to view a pop-up window showing a preview of the linked site. Now it is possible to view each site without leaving the results page.

Figure 2.5 Google Instant Preview

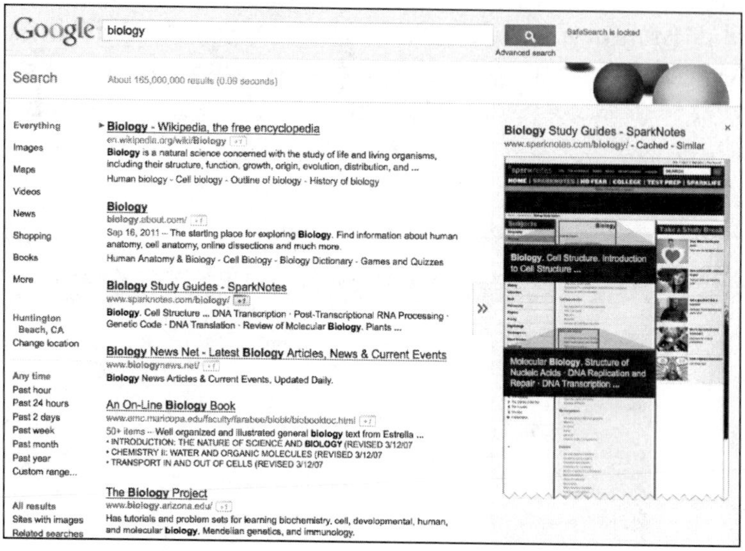

Google Instant Preview in the Classroom

Take your students to the computer lab and show them how to narrow their searches using Google Instant Preview.

1. Have students open Google and type *cell structure* into the search box.

2. Challenge students to find (without using Instant Preview) three websites that provide a detailed labeled diagram of a cell. Use a timer or stopwatch to time how long it takes students to find three suitable diagrams.

3. Show students how to use Google Instant Preview, and then time them as they search for *atomic structure* and find three websites that provide detailed, labeled diagrams of the structure of an atom. Were they able to find them faster?

Related Searches

Once you have a page of search results, click *Show search tools* or *More search tools* in the left sidebar and then click *Related searches*.

Figure 2.6 Related Searches in the Left Sidebar

All results
Sites with images
Related searches
Timeline
Dictionary
Reading level
Nearby
Translated foreign
    pages

Google displays a list of possible searches related to your original search. These options can help broaden your search or help you focus on what you really want. A related search can also give information about topics that are interconnected with your original search. In the example below, a related search for *onomatopoeia* lists other types of figurative language.

Figure 2.7 Related Search

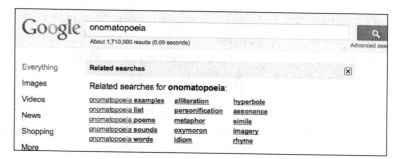

Find Within Page

After searching for and selecting a website, it is sometimes difficult to find the information you are looking for within the page. Press *Command+F* (Mac) or *Control+F* (PC) on your keyboard to open a search box in your browser. Type in a word or phrase to see it highlighted within the displayed page. While this tool is part of the browser and not Google, it can save a great deal of time.

Search by Type of Content

Google searches can be narrowed based on the type of information you are looking for, such as news, books, images, or video. These tools, available at the top of the search screen and in the left sidebar, allow searches for specific types of information with one click.

Google News Search

Google News searches news sources all over the world, both print and online. Enter your search terms in the search bar and click *News* in the left sidebar. Use the filters in the left sidebar to narrow the search results by time: *Past hour*, *Past 24 hours*, *Past week*, *Past month*, etc. Use *Custom range…* to search news sources within a specific time period. To access historical news sources, click *Archive*.

Google News Search in the Classroom

Use Google News to access primary source information for use in the classroom. Search any historical or current event and use the time filters in the left sidebar to specify the time period for articles. The example below shows a news search for "Apollo 11," filtered by year, that returned news articles originally published during the week of the first moon landing.

Figure 2.8 Google News Search

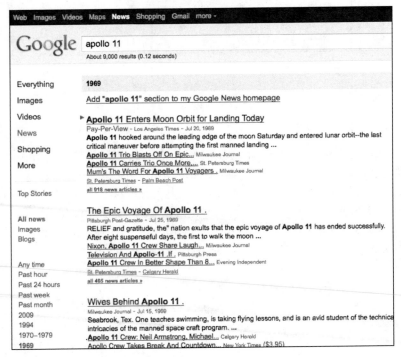

Tip Larger publications, such as the *New York Times* or *Chicago Tribune*, will often charge a small fee to view older articles, but many smaller, local newspapers' archives are available at no cost.

Figure 2.9 Google News Search: Newspaper Article

Google Books

Google Books allows students to search libraries instead of the entire Web. Google has made millions of volumes of text searchable online, and in many cases, they are available in full-text versions. Snippets and previews are available as well. Google Books is a great research tool for students. To see the detail of a Google Books search, try this search related to cell division.

Try It

Google Books Search

1. Type "cell division" into the Google search box.

2. At the top of the page, click *more*, then *Books*.

3. Click the link to *The cell cycle: principles of control*, which will open the Google Books viewer.

4. To search within the book, look for the *Search in this book* search box on the left; type in "eukaryotes" and click *go*. Pages referencing eukaryotes are displayed.

5. Click a page number to view the referenced page. Search terms are highlighted within the text to make finding relevant information easier.

Figure 2.10 Google Books Search

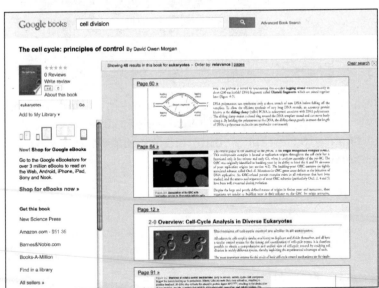

Google Images

Google Images searches for visual images, such as photographs, illustrations, and diagrams. Search results are displayed as thumbnail images. Hold your cursor over a thumbnail to see information such as the name of the file, size of the image, and the website on which it is hosted. Click a thumbnail to open a preview pane with more information about the image.

Figure 2.11 Google Images Search

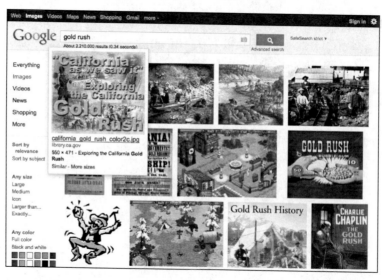

In the preview pane, the image is displayed in a window over the website in which it was found. In the right sidebar, click *Website for this image* to view the website, or click *Full-size image* to see the larger version.

Figure 2.12 Google Images Preview Pane

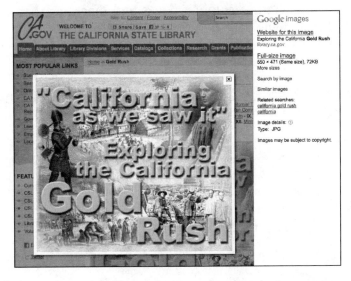

A basic image search will return many images, but you may not see exactly what you are looking for. Use the image filtering tools in the left sidebar to help you narrow your search even further. *Sort by subject* will display images in groups.

Figure 2.13 Google Images Search: Sort by Subject

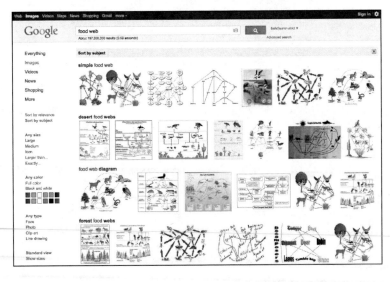

Images can also be sorted by size, color, or type. The *Line drawing* filter will often return coloring pages and diagrams that can be printed for students.

Figure 2.14 Google Images Search: Line Drawing

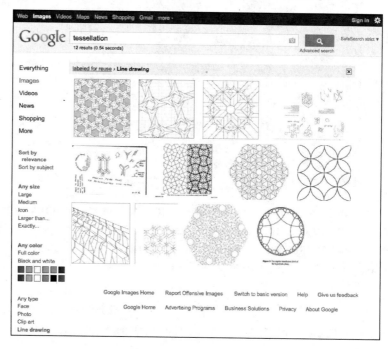

Usage Rights Image Search

A Google Images search can provide valuable teaching tools for use in the classroom, and students often use this type of search to find pictures to paste into reports and projects. But how do you know if you are allowed to copy and reuse an image?

1. In a Google Images search results page, click *Advanced search* (just below the search button).

2. In the *Usage rights* menu, select *Only images labeled for reuse* to see images that are licensed for use as they appear. If you are looking for images that you can change or modify, select *Modification*.

3. Click *Search images* to see images that you can copy and use in the classroom.

Figure 2.15 Usage Rights Image Search

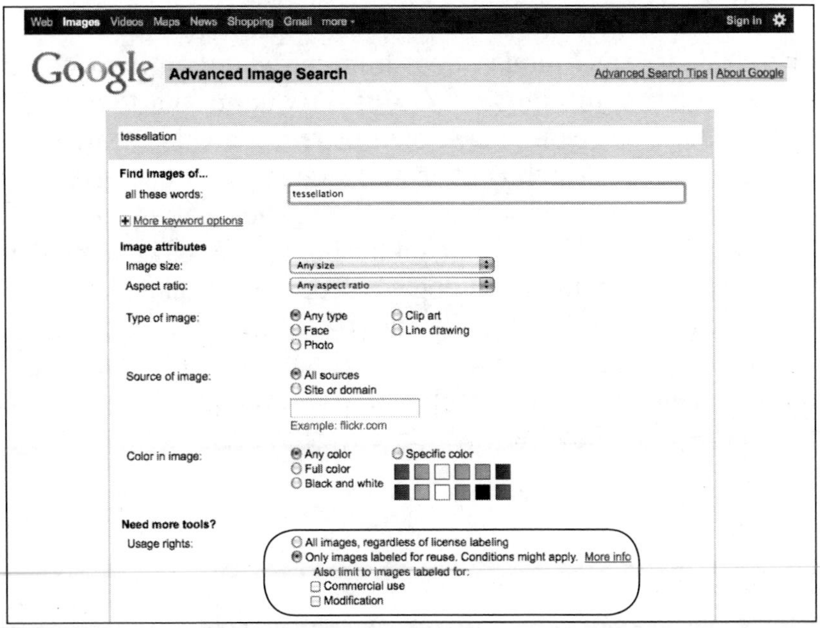

Figure 2.16 Usage Rights Image Search Results

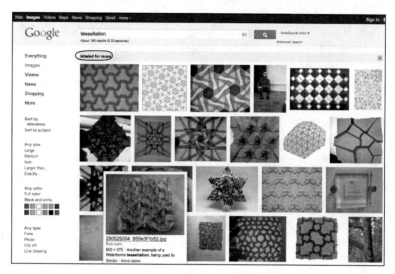

Google Videos

Google Videos search finds videos from anywhere on the Web. If you have ever spent hours on *YouTube®* trying to find the perfect instructional video, you know how frustrating a video search can be. Google Video search is plain and simple. In a Google search page, click on *Videos*, located on the navigation bar at the top of the browser screen. (Depending on the browser, it may be found in the *More* pull-down menu.) Google Videos is an excellent resource for the classroom teacher in finding instructional materials. For example, Board Policy in my school district requires the acknowledgement of Constitution Day. A Google Videos search for "Constitution Day" turned up a vast number of videos on the topic.

Figure 2.17 Google Videos Search

Google | constitution day

Search | About 38,400 results (0.08 seconds)

Everything
Images
Maps
Videos
News
Shopping
More

Any duration
Short (0–4 min.)
Medium (4–20 min.)
Long (20+ min.)

Any time
Past hour
Past 24 hours
Past week
Past month
Past year
Custom range...

Any quality
High quality

All videos
Closed captioned

Ads

It's Your **Constitution** - Learn to love it more | pjtv.com
www.pjtv.com/FreedomsCharter
Watch Freedom's Charter on PJTV.

When Is **Constitution Day** | Ask.com
www.ask.com/When+Is+Constitution+Day
Look up When Is **Constitution Day** Get the Best Answers Now!

constitution day | ShopAtHome.com
www.shopathome.com
Savings at **Constitution** Center **constitution day**

National **Constitution** Center: **Constitution Day**
constitutioncenter.org
Jun 3, 2009
Resources to help celebrate **Constitution Day** and develop habits of citizenship in a new generation of Americans ...

Constitution Day (September 18, 2006)
youtube.com
Sep 19, 2007 - 7 min - Uploaded by constitutionday
Constitution Day video preamble by General Colin Powell.
www.constitutionday.com

US **Constitution Day**
schooltube.com
Sep 13, 2011 - 6 min
Rob Richardson introduces US **Constitution Day** Lesson for SAUSD schools

The Preamble: **Constitution Day**
schooltube.com

Tip

If your school blocks *YouTube*®, filter video searches by *Source*. *SchoolTube*®, *TeacherTube*®, and *PBS* are usually school-friendly.

Search Filters

Google's search filters narrow search results by showing only specific types of information. Click on *More search tools* in the left sidebar to display filter options. The filters available may change depending on the search terms entered and the filters already being used.

Dictionary

Enter a word into the Google search box and click *Dictionary* to display definitions and usage examples. Click the speaker icon to hear the pronunciation of the word. Google also displays synonyms and related phrases.

Figure 2.18 Dictionary Search

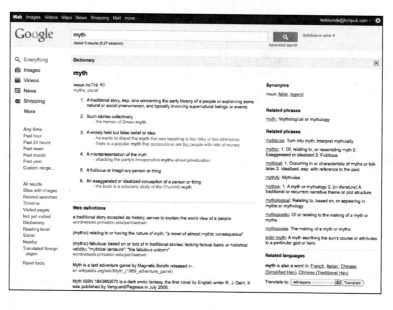

In the Classroom: Dictionary Filter

Students can use the Google Dictionary filter to find the meaning and usage of vocabulary words and hear them pronounced correctly. This is especially useful for unfamiliar and hard-to-pronounce academic vocabulary terms such as *isosceles* (mathematics), *Persephone* (history), *Jabberwocky* (language arts), or *paramecium* (science).

Reading Level

A Reading Level search displays results that can be narrowed by Basic, Intermediate, or Advanced reading levels. Click on a reading level to display only results at that reading level.

Figure 2.19 Reading Level Search

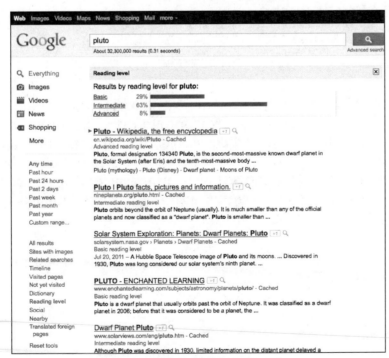

Google Scholar

Google Scholar searches journals and publications and returns links to scholarly articles and court documents. This tool is available under the *More* pull down menu at the top of the Google search page. The *Cited by* and *Related articles* links under each listing will return lists of related works. *Library search* indicates which local libraries have a copy of the listed book.

Figure 2.20 Google Scholar Search

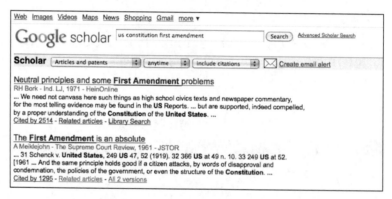

A Google Scholar search can return great primary source information for use in the classroom. Search for court cases, such as Brown v. Board of Education, to find original court documents, and search for inventors, such as Thomas Edison or Nikola Tesla, to find their original patents. Use the first pull-down menu in Google Scholar to search by type of document, such as U.S. court documents or patents.

Figure 2.21 Google Scholar Search By Type of Document

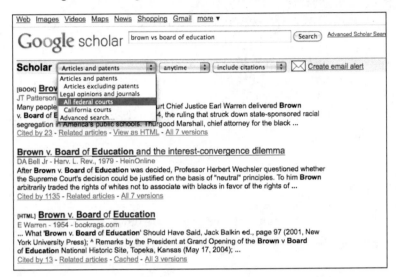

Advanced Search

The amount of information returned in a basic Google search can be overwhelming. Use Advanced Search to eliminate unwanted results or search for specific types of files. Access the Advanced Search option by clicking on the gear icon in the upper-right corner of any Google search page and selecting *Advanced Search*.

Eliminate Unwanted Results

Often search terms relate to more than one subject and many of the returned links may be irrelevant to you. For example, if you are looking for information for a social studies unit on the Gold Rush and you search for *forty-niners*, many of the links will be related to the football team. Use Advanced Search to get more links related to social studies and fewer links related to professional sports.

Eliminate Unwanted Results

1. Type "forty-niners" into the search box and click the *Advanced search* button.

2. Type "NFL, football" in the box labeled *But don't show pages that have....*

3. Click *Advanced Search* in the lower right corner to see search results.

Figure 2.22 Advanced Search, Eliminate Unwanted Results

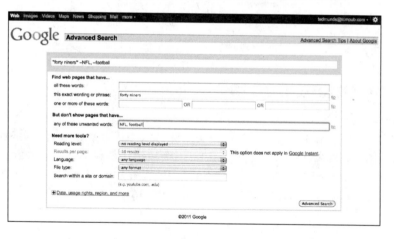

File Type Search

Searching by file type allows you to search for files according to the programs that have been used to create them. In the *Advanced search* menu, pull down the *File type* menu to choose the type of file you would like to see. You can search for *Microsoft PowerPoint®* slideshows, *Google Earth* .kmz and .kml files, *Microsoft Excel®* spreadsheets, *Adobe Acrobat®* PDF files, *Microsoft Word* documents, *Shockwave Flash®* animations, and more.

Figure 2.23 File Type Search

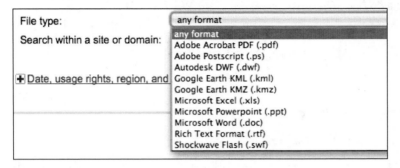

Usage Rights Search

It is very important to consider fair use and copyright when searching for information on the Internet. Google searches will nearly always display work that has been created by someone else, and just because it is being used in the classroom does not automatically mean you are free to use the information. This myth must be dispelled: *Just because it is on the World Wide Web does not mean it can be copied.* Many people upload their work because they love to share. Others do so out of convenience but do not want it to be used unless it is paid for. How can you tell if you can use something in your classroom that you find on the Web? Try a *Usage rights* search.

In the Advanced Search menu, click *Date, usage rights, region, and more* at the bottom to open the menu. Use the pull down *Usage rights* menu to choose the types of sites you would like to see.

Figure 2.24 Usage Rights Search

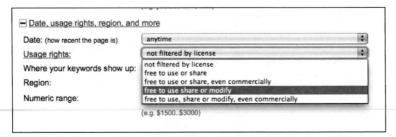

Tip Choose *free to use, share, or modify* to see files you can customize for your classroom.

? Reflection Questions

1. How are your students currently doing their research? How could they enhance their research process with the use of Google's search features?

2. What do you need to do to teach your students to properly research using the Internet?

3. Think about what you are requiring when it comes to sources in a bibliography. Do you need to provide training for your students in how to cite Internet sources?

Chapter 3

Google Docs™

While most of us think of Google as a search engine, that's just the tip of the iceberg. There are many powerful applications available from Google for free. Google Docs includes a word processor, presentation editor, form creator, and spreadsheet program that are not only easy to use, but enable users to create and share online. With Google Docs, it is possible to create brand new documents or upload material previously created in *Microsoft Word*, *PowerPoint*®, or *Excel*®. Everything is stored online, so it can be accessed from any computer that is connected to the Internet. The real magic for students is that all Google Docs can be shared, both with the teacher and with other students, creating instant opportunities for collaborative learning. The following tools are available with a free Google account:

- Documents
- Presentations
- Drawings
- Forms
- Spreadsheets

Google Accounts

In order to take advantage of Google's productivity tools, a Google account is necessary. With an existing email address, it is easy to set up a free Google account. You can create as many Google accounts as you have email addresses.

Note: See Chapter 5, *Using Google in the Classroom*, for tips on setting up student accounts.

Try It

Set Up a Google Account

1. Go to the Google home page and click on *Sign in* at the top right corner.

2. Click on *Create an account for free* or *Sign up for a new Google Account* and complete the form.

Figure 3.1 Google Accounts Creation

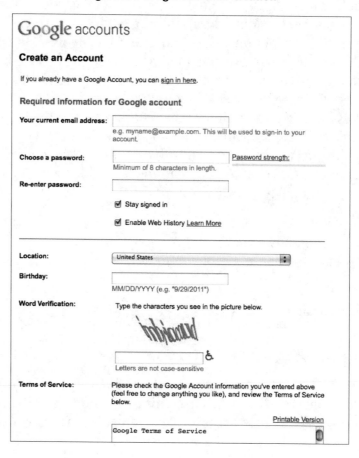

3. Go to your email account, open the confirmation email, and click the link to confirm your account. You can now access Google tools when you are signed in to your Google account.

4. Go to docs.google.com or click *Documents* under the *More* pull-down menu in the Google toolbar to see your new Google Docs home page. Bookmark this page; it is the starting point for using many Google tools.

 If you ever get stuck, the *Help* option in Google Docs is incredibly useful. There are help videos, as well as "testimonies" from other Google users.

Google Documents

Google Documents is a word processing application that offers a few different fonts, some simple formatting, and the ability to insert pictures, tables, highlights, and comments. It is not as robust as the word processing program that is downloaded on your computer, but it gets the job done.

Using Google Documents is an easy alternative to emailing yourself dozens of projects that you need to finish at home. For example, if I am working on my newsletter at school and need to get home to take my daughters to soccer practice, I would normally attach it to an email and send it to myself so I can download it to my home computer, finish it, and email it back to myself. This requires that I remember which revision is which, not to mention being able to find it in my inbox. Instead, I can upload my newsletter to Google Docs so that it is in The Cloud and accessible to me at home.

This portability is great for students as well. No more lost homework due to crashed computers; all their work is safe in Google Docs. They can access it from any Internet-enabled computer—from home, the library, computer lab, or Grandma's house.

Try It

Create a Word-Processing Document with Google Documents

1. Sign into your Google account and go to your Google Docs home page (docs.google.com).

2. Click on the *Create* button menu and select *Document* from the pull-down menu.

Figure 3.2 Create a New Document

3. Name your document by clicking *Untitled document* at the top of the page and typing in the new name.

Figure 3.3 Google Document Screen

4. Type some text into the body of the document.

5. Google Docs saves your document automatically every few minutes. Close the document and return to your Google Docs home page. Look for the name of the document you just created. You can now access this file from any Internet-enabled computer by signing in to your Google account.

Uploading Files to Google Docs

In addition to creating a document from scratch, you can upload files from your computer to Google Docs. The *Upload* button in the Google Docs home page allows you to send files from your computer to your Google Docs account. In the *Upload* pull-down menu, click *Files* and select the files you want to upload. Even easier, just drag the files from your computer onto the Google Docs homepage and they will upload automatically. Uploaded files are converted into Google Docs format and appear in your Google Docs homepage.

Figure 3.4 Upload Menu in Google Docs

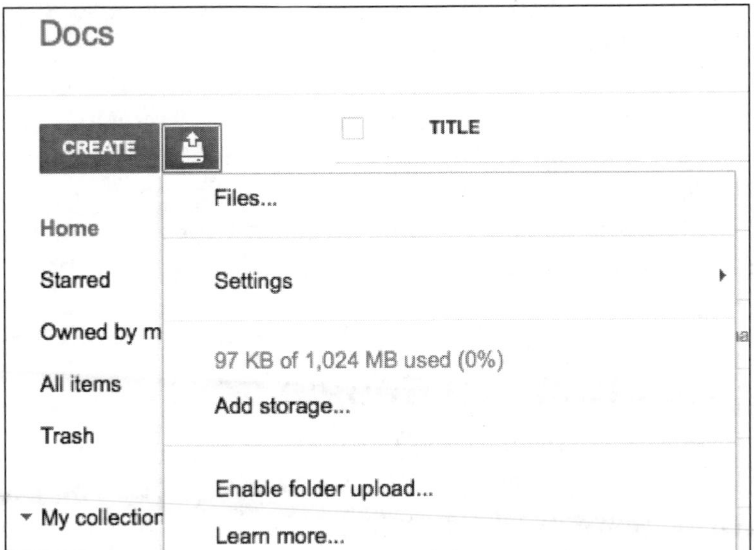

Tip There is a 1MB limit on files uploaded to Google Docs.

Downloading Files to Your Computer

To save a file from Google Docs to your computer, first open the file in Google Docs. In the *File* menu, select *Download as* to save the document to your computer in the format of your choice. To save a file for printing or sharing (that cannot be changed), save it as a PDF document (readable in *Adobe Acrobat*®). To save a file that you can edit on your computer when you are offline, save it as a *Microsoft Word* document.

Google Documents is a basic word processing program. If you need to add clip art, Word Art®, etc., save your Google document to your computer in *Microsoft Word* format. Then, you can open it in *Microsoft Word* and add the extra bells and whistles. This book was written using Google Docs. Having this book in The Cloud allowed me to sit on the couch in the living room, write a few words from coffee shops and other places with free Wi-Fi, use my daughter's or my husband's computer, my office computer, etc. However, when all was said and done, and it was time to insert screenshots and any other graphics, I downloaded the book into my computer in *Microsoft Word*. In order to really manipulate graphics and "play" with format, you need a bit more power in your word processing program than Google Documents provides.

Presentations in Google Docs

Google Presentation allows you to create a slideshow in The Cloud. This is another opportunity for you and your students to work on a project from anywhere there is Internet access. Creating slideshows in Google Presentation is very similar to *Microsoft PowerPoint*® in the way that you can create slides, move them around, change their backgrounds, and more. You can insert images and videos using the *Insert* menu and add speaker notes as well. Files can be uploaded from and downloaded to a computer.

Try It

Create a Google Presentation

1. Sign in to your Google account and go to your Google Docs homepage.

2. Click on the *Create* button and select *Presentation*.

3. Name your presentation by clicking *Untitled Presentation* and typing in the new name.

4. Use the presentation tools in the top toolbar or pull-down menus to insert text and images.

Figure 3.5 Presentation Tools

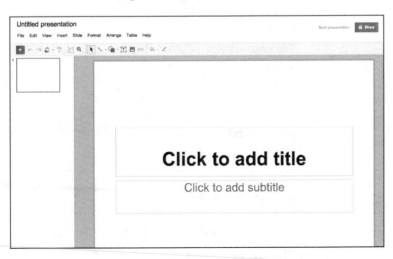

5. Right-click on the slide thumbnails in the left sidebar to open a slide management menu where you can insert, delete, move, duplicate, copy, and paste slides. You can also drag and drop slides in the left sidebar.

Figure 3.6 Presentation Slide Management Menu

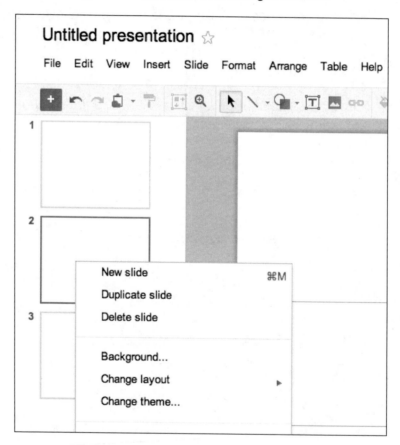

6. To begin your presentation, click *Start presentation* at the top of the screen. To end the presentation, close the browser window.

Uploading and Downloading a Presentation

Just as you can upload a *Microsoft Word*® document into Google Docs, you can also upload a *Microsoft PowerPoint*™ presentation from your computer. The formatting may be slightly altered, but it allows you to work on your presentation in Google Presentation and bring it back into *Microsoft PowerPoint* later if that is the format you like best. To print a presentation, download it as a PDF file.

 In Google Presentations, when you select *Google Image Search* in the *Insert Image* menu, all images displayed are licensed for commercial reuse with modification, so you can use them in your documents and presentations without worrying about copyright infringement.

Google Drawing

Create graphics with Google Drawing quickly and easily and paste them into documents and presentations. Use the drawing tools to insert lines, shapes, and text. Use the Web clipboard to copy the entire drawing and paste it into a document, presentation, blog, or website.

Figure 3.7 Google Drawing

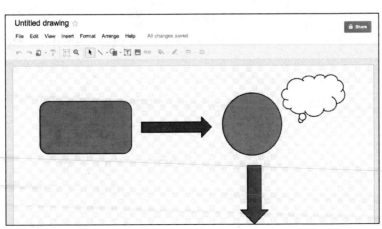

Create a Venn Diagram with Google Drawing

1. In the Google Docs home page, click on the *Create* button and select *Drawing*. Name your drawing at the top of the page by clicking *Untitled Drawing* at the top and typing in the new name.

2. In the *Shapes* menu, select the circle. Click and drag in the drawing window to draw a large circle. Drag one of the white squares in the corner of the frame to resize the circle.

Figure 3.8 Google Drawing Shapes Menu

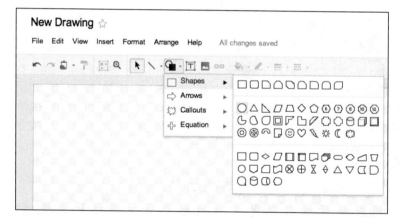

3. Right-click on the circle or use the *Edit* pull-down menu to Select *Copy* to copy the circle, then select *Paste* to paste a new, second circle in the drawing.

Figure 3.9 Google Drawing Edit Pop-up Menu

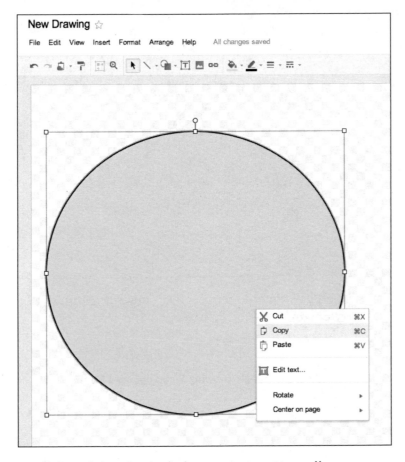

4. Click and drag both circles to create a Venn diagram.

5. Click each circle once, then use the *Fill color* menu to set both circles to *Transparent*.

Figure 3.10 Google Drawing Fill Color Menu

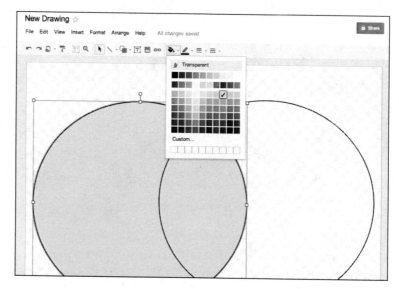

6. In the *Web clipboard* menu, select *Copy entire drawing to web clipboard*.

Figure 3.11 Google Drawing Web Clipboard Menu

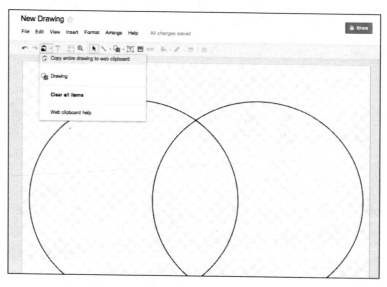

7. Go back to the Google Docs home page and create or open the document or presentation into which you would like to place the Venn diagram.

8. In the *Web clipboard* menu, select the name of the drawing to paste it into your document or presentation.

Forms in Google Docs

Google Forms collect information from multiple people through an online response form. Responders do not need a Google account to fill out a form. Responses are collected automatically in an online spreadsheet connected to the form. Charts and graphs can be created from the collected data with one click, and responses can then be downloaded into *Microsoft Excel*®.

Google Forms is a huge timesaver. Send a form to parents to collect contact information and volunteer availability. Create an online book report form for students to complete at home or in the computer lab. Give students a form to record their progress on a long-term assignment. In each case, the data collected is automatically entered in a spreadsheet for your use.

Items in Google Forms

Google Forms provides a number of question types so you can customize your forms.

- A *Text* item allows responders to enter short text.

- A *Paragraph Text* item allows responders to enter longer text.

- A *Multiple Choice* item allows responders to choose one response from a list.

- A *Checkboxes* item allows responders to choose multiple responses on a list.

- A *Choose from a list* item allows responders to choose a response from a drop-down list.

- A *Scale* item allows responders to choose a response on a scale.

- A *Grid* item allows responders to choose multiple responses from a grid.

Figure 3.12 Google Forms Item Types

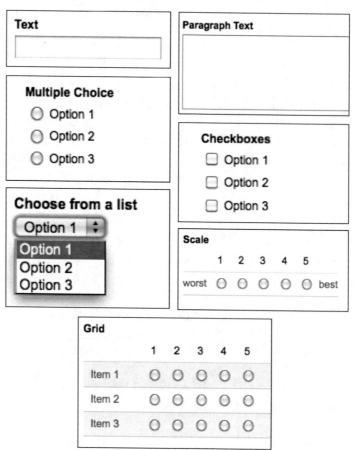

Try It

Create a Form in Google Forms

1. Sign into your Google account and go to the Google Docs home page.

2. Click on the *Create* button and select *Form.*

3. Name your form by clicking *Untitled form* and typing in the new name.

4. Use *Theme* to alter the form's appearance. Select the theme you like by clicking it and then click *Apply* to save the changes.

Figure 3.13 Google Forms Theme Menu

5. Use the *Add item* pull-down menu to insert items in the form. Enter information in each item.

Figure 3.14 Google Forms Add Item Menu

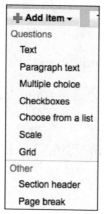

6. Save your form to the Google Docs home page by clicking *Save* in the top-right corner.

7. Click on the name of your form in the Google Docs home page to access the form spreadsheet. To see the form itself, use the *Form* pull-down menu to select *Go to live form*. To edit the form, select *Edit form*.

Figure 3.15 Edit Form

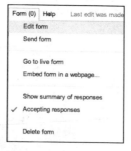

Sharing a Google Form

There are numerous ways to share a form. If responses are required from a specific audience or group of people, such as parents, students, or staff members, emailing the link is the most user-friendly method of sharing. When you are editing the form, a Web address is displayed at the bottom of the form. This URL can be copied and pasted into an email, or, to reach a wider audience, it can be posted on a website or blog.

Figure 3.16 Form URL

You can view the published form here: https://docs.google.com/spreadsheet/viewform?formkey=dEVuSFF1WFZ2ck1NdTE0Z1VVTjRlVXc6MQ

The form can also be sent by clicking *Email this form* (at the top of the form) to open the form-sharing window. Enter the email addresses in the *to:* box.

Figure 3.17 *Email this form* Window

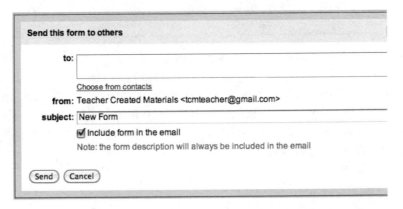

If you choose *Email as attachment,* the form is attached as a *Microsoft Excel®* spreadsheet, which makes it difficult for recipients to fill out the form. It is better to email or post the link in most cases.

Form Spreadsheets

Once people start filling out a form, all of the responses are automatically entered into a spreadsheet. This spreadsheet is accessible from the Google Docs home page. Data can be organized and analyzed as it would in *Microsoft Excel®*. Google Form spreadsheets also include one-click graphs and charts.

Figure 3.18 Google Forms Spreadsheet

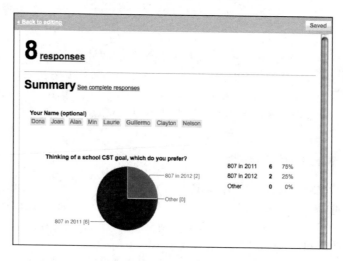

With the *Summary of Responses* feature, Google Docs instantly creates charts summarizing all of the data collected via the form. Text responses are listed as they are entered. A graph charting the number of daily responses to the form can also be displayed. This feature can be accessed in the *Form* pull-down menu under *Show summary of responses.*

Figure 3.19 Summary of Responses

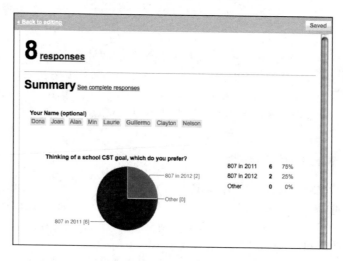

Google Spreadsheets

Google Spreadsheets lets you create, update, modify, and share spreadsheets online. Google Spreadsheets is compatible with *Microsoft Excel®* and offers typical spreadsheet features, such as the ability to add, delete, and sort rows and columns. This application also allows multiple users to collaborate on a spreadsheet in real time. Basic charts, such as pie, bar, and scatter charts, can be created from Google Spreadsheets data. You can share a spreadsheet with your students and allow them to input data to a classroom file, and then they can analyze data and create charts and graphs.

Create a Spreadsheet in Google Spreadsheets

1. Sign into your Google account and go to the Google Docs home page.

2. Click on the *Create* button and select *Spreadsheet*.

3. Name the spreadsheet by clicking *Untitled Spreadsheet* and typing in the new name.

4. Use the spreadsheet tools to create the spreadsheet, just as you would in *Microsoft Excel®*.

5. Create a chart by clicking on *Insert* and selecting *Chart* in the toolbar. Choose the type of chart or graph you want and customize by clicking the *Customize* tab.

Figure 3.20 Spreadsheets Chart Window

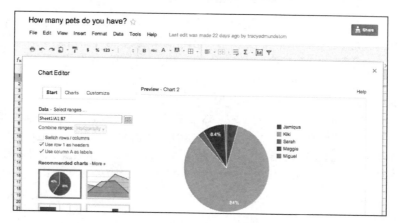

6. To share your spreadsheet with others, click the *Share* button in the upper right corner of the screen and enter their email addresses.

7. To save the spreadsheet to your computer, click on the *File* menu, select *Download as*, and choose a format.

 Tip Share your spreadsheet with colleagues or students and you can chat with them when they are online at the same time. Just click on their names in the right-hand window.

Figure 3.21 Chat in Spreadsheets

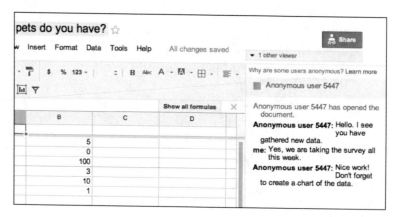

Sharing and Collaborating in Google Docs

Perhaps the greatest reason to use Google in the classroom is the ability to share. Many people can collaborate on one document without the need to email back and forth. Students can work from both school and home, since all they need is a computer with an Internet connection. They can share Google Docs with their teacher, their classmates, and their parents.

In order for multiple people to collaborate on a single document, each person must have a Google account. Everyone that opens a standalone Google account has a Gmail address that can be used for sharing Google Docs. Everyone the document is shared with receives an email inviting him or her to access the document. If the document is shared with someone that does not have a Google account, that person is invited to create an account when he or she receives the invitation.

There are two ways to share documents with other Google account holders. People can be invited as *viewers*, which means they cannot change anything in the document, or they can be invited as *editors* so they can collaborate in the creating and editing processes.

Try It

Share a Document

1. In the Google Docs home page, open the document you want to share.

2. Click *Share* in the upper right-hand corner of the document.

3. In the pop-up window, under *Add people*, type the email addresses of the people with whom you want to share the document.

Figure 3.22 Sharing Settings Window

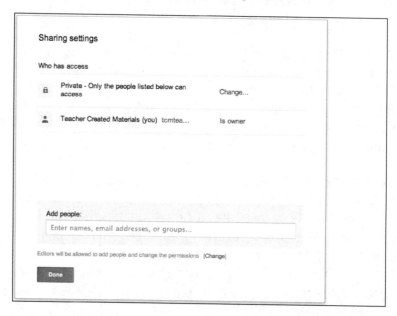

4. To the right of their names, choose *Can view* or *Can edit*.

5. Check the box next to *Notify people via email*. Click *Add message* if you want to type in a message.

6. Click *Share & save* to share your document.

7. After you share the document, the pop-up window will display a list of the people who can view and edit the document.

8. The current privacy setting is displayed at the top of the pop-up window. Click *Change...* to make the document private or public.

A copy of a document can be emailed by selecting *Email as attachment* and choosing a format. This is a great option for sharing with those who do not have a Google account. The document can be emailed to all the people sharing it by selecting *Email collaborators*.

Tip With the advent of Google+, an online social network, there are two *Share* buttons available to you when you create or edit a document. The *Share* button on the Navigation bar is to be used only if you want to share in Google+. Read more about Google+ on page 75.

Organizing Collections

Sharing Google Docs with a single class of students, a large number of students over multiple class periods, or an entire school or district staff can cause organization to spiral out of control easily. Here are some tips to keep your Google Docs organized.

Each time a document is created or another user shares a document with you, the individual document appears in the main Google Docs folder. There may be more than a hundred documents in the main folder at one time. This makes it difficult to scroll and search to find a document, so create collections to organize documents. In Google Docs, a folder is called a *collection*. Create a new collection by selecting *Collection* in the *Create* menu. Then drag docs from the main menu into the new collection.

Figure 3.23 Create Menu

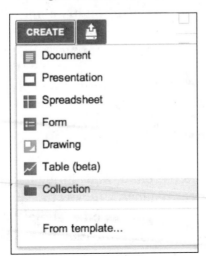

Once documents have been placed in collection folders, they still appear in the main menu. They do not disappear when they are moved. In fact, every time a document is edited, it reappears in the main Google Docs page. To keep docs organized, "hide" the documents in the main menu once they are in folders. To do this, right-click on the document you want to hide and select *Don't show in home*. The document name disappears from view. Fear not, they are tucked away safely in their collections. To hide multiple docs at once, hold the shift key while selecting them and drag the whole selection into a collection.

Google Earth

Google Earth can bring the world to life for students. In Google Earth, thousands of high-resolution images of our planet taken from space have been joined together onto a virtual globe. Google Earth allows users to "fly" to any place on Earth and view these images at almost any resolution. Unlike other Google tools, Google Earth does need to be downloaded onto a computer. The latest version of Google Earth can be downloaded at http://www.earth.google.com.

When Google Earth is opened, a window appears showing Earth as seen from space. When a city or country name is typed into the *Fly to* box, Google Earth "flies" to that location. The navigation tools allow users to move around and explore the earth.

In the *Layers* panel, various layers can be turned on, such as *Borders and Labels* and *Places*, that display lines and icons on Earth. The 3D Buildings layer contains 3D models of many famous landmarks such as the Statue of Liberty, the Eiffel Tower, and the ruins at Pompei. Users can zoom in and use the navigation tools to virtually "walk" on, around, and through many locations and buildings. Google Earth allows students to experience geography, history, literature, science, or any other subject area in an exciting and engaging way. Below are some examples of how to use Google Earth in the classroom.

- Fly over a metropolitan city such as New York City or London to view the 3D shapes that architects use in real-world buildings.

- Turn on the *Weather* layers to compare and contrast weather patterns over deserts, forests, and oceans.

- Fly to a historical site, such as the Coliseum in Rome or Windsor Castle in London, and have students virtually reenact an important historical event.

- Use the ruler tool to measure distances between cities and plan efficient transportation routes.

- Fly to a body of water, such as the Mississippi River or Lake Victoria, to examine what the habitat looks like near the water and farther away.

Figure 3.24 Google Earth

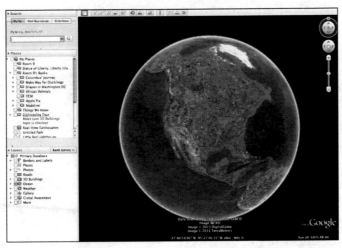

Google Lit Trips

The easiest way to get started using Google Earth in the classroom is with Google Lit Trips (http://www.googlelittrips.org). Created by Jerome Burg, a 34-year veteran high-school English teacher, Google Lit Trips are the ultimate way to take students into literature and beyond.

> GoogleLitTrips.com is flat out a fantastic project with deep examples of the way technology can be meaningfully integrated into the curriculum. Too often in technology there is a lamentable lag between promise and classroom realization. Jerome Burg closed that gap with GoogleLitTrips. Classical works, modern literature, and wordless primary illustrations are given new life, new access, and a critical new perspective for classrooms. Media, literature, and the earth itself converge here in one of the most exemplary technology integration sites on the educational World Wide Web.

(Hall Davidson, Director of Discovery Educator Network)

Figure 3.25 Google Lit Trips

Each Lit Trip consists of a .kmz or .kml file that can be downloaded into a computer and opened with Google Earth. When students open the *Grapes of Wrath* Lit Trip .kmz file in Google Earth, they see satellite imagery of the globe. The image spins before it stops on California. Key locations are marked with placemarks to relate to each day of the Joads' travels. The sidebar on the left of the screen organizes all the geographic information by chapter as well. By using the tools in Google Earth, students can zoom in for a closer look or tilt the view to see the terrain or buildings in 3D. They can fly from place to place along a virtual Route 66. By clicking on a placemark, students open a pop-up window embedded with supplementary information. Most pop-ups include photos, maps, drawings, or text, and often have questions to encourage students to think about the story.

Google Lit Trips began with a few pieces of literature in 2007 and, with the help of many contributing educators, has grown to more than 30 lessons. Additional .kmz and .kml files can be found using Google Advanced Search file type search (see *The Power of Google Search* on page 26).

Google+

Google's goal with Google+ is to connect people via the Web like they connect in the real world. We share different things with people, depending on who they are, so why shouldn't we be able to pick and choose with whom we want to share online? One of the biggest advantages of Google+ is privacy. In most social networking sites, everything is shared with everyone. With Google+, you can choose what to share with whom by creating *Circles*. You may create a circle for your friends, another for your students, another for colleagues, and perhaps a circle of folks you want to "follow" but would prefer that they never know a thing about you. Users seem to be responding well to Google+; it took only 16 days to reach 10 million users, as many as *Facebook* and *Twitter* did in nearly three years (Butcher 2011).

It may be the level of privacy afforded by Google+ that is the key to making this a useful tool for schools. Some educators use *Facebook* or *Twitter* in the classrooms, however, they are not ideal in a school setting. It is very difficult to guarantee any sort of private conversation through social networking sites. Google+ is built around what Vincent Mo of Google calls "targeted sharing." He explains, "*On Google+, anyone can add me to their circles, and they never see more than what I share with them. It's as easy as not adding them to a circle. That means people can add me all they want. If I post something private, I'll only post it to a circle, and they won't see it*" (Mo 2011).

Features of Google+

Google+ is constantly changing. Here are a few of the key features:

- **Google+ Circles:** Google+ allows users to create groups called *Circles* to organize friends, colleagues, relatives, and professional contacts in specific groups. People can be assigned to more than one circle. For example, I have a few friends that are in the educational technology field. They are in my "Friend" circle as well as my "Ed Tech" circle. This way, if I post to the Ed Tech circle, both my colleagues and my friends will see my technology post, but if I want to post pictures of my children, the entire Ed Tech circle does not get to see them. Every time I post something, I can choose to share it with one circle, multiple circles, or even the "public" circle where everyone can see it.

- **Google+ Messenger:** Messenger allows multiple users to chat in real time. It is like having a group text within a Google+ group. It makes it very convenient to get the word out to a group of people, as long as they are all using Google+. (Note that this feature is constantly changing.)

Figure 3.26 Google+ Circles

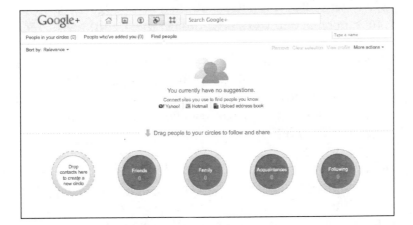

- **Google+ Hangouts:** Hangouts allow for face-to-face online collaboration with up to ten different people using video. Each hangout is given a particular URL that can be shared via Google+, email, or the Web. To join in on the video conversation, Google+ members just click the link.

- **Google+ Sparks:** The idea behind Sparks is to "spark" a conversation with others about a topic that interests you. Click the *Sparks* button to find "stuff you're interested in." Type an interest in the Sparks search box and Google+ provides up-to-date articles that you can easily share with your circles.

Google+ in Education

Google+ can be used to create the ultimate Professional Learning Community (PLC); the ultimate collaborative tool for teaching and learning. Many see it as a game changer in education. The Apps User Group published a list of possible classroom uses early on in the life of Google+ (Curts 2011).

- **Student work groups:** Circles can be set up for student collaboration. Students could then use Hangouts as a virtual meeting place to work on a project, peer edit, revise, etc.

- **Online teaching:** Hangouts can be used as a virtual classroom to teach students online. Possibilities include after-school tutoring sessions, exam review sessions, or video and slideshow sharing. Currently, a Hangout may consist of ten people at a time.

- **Staff development:** Hangouts lend themselves to staff development. Discussions can be held via Hangout, and with the use of webcams, it's the next best thing to being there. Individual teachers could use Sparks to keep up to date on the latest content area information or educational technology developments.

- **School Community:** Videos from school events such as drama, sports, awards ceremonies, and assemblies can be automatically uploaded to Google+ and shared with Circles. Circles of parents or community members can be created for this purpose. Instant upload will make putting such events on the school website an easy, one-step process.

❓ Reflection Questions

1. How could you use one Google tool to increase your professional productivity or make your work life easier?

2. How could you use one Google tool to increase student achievement or address standards? Consider your own classroom as well as your school's goals and strategic plan.

3. Name two groups of people with whom you could improve communication by sharing Google Docs.

Chapter 4

Google Sites | Search

Google Sites is an easy-to-use, free website builder with no knowledge of programming or coding required. One Google account can be used to create multiple sites. All these sites are located in The Cloud for easy access. Google Sites can be shared with colleagues, students, or anyone with a Google account so that the site can be a collaborative project. For example, you can create a classroom site, one site for each subject area, a professional development site, or a personal site. Have your students create a website for a book character or a Greek god.

Google Sites allow users to create multiple website pages and embed rich content, images, and video in those pages. Google tools such as Google Calendars, Google Docs, *YouTube* videos, and *Picasa* photo albums can be embedded directly into Google Sites. Google Sites maintain revisions, just like Google Docs and allows users to revert to an earlier revision at any time.

Creating a Site

Google Sites provide WYSIWYG ("What You See Is What You Get") site creation so there is no need for complicated computer codes. It only takes a few clicks to create a website.

Create a Classroom Website

1. Sign in to your Google account.

2. Go to http://sites.google.com or click *Sites* at the top of the Google Docs home page.

3. Click on the *Create* button.

4. Choose a layout. Google Sites has several layouts and designs to choose from. The template gallery offers pre-designed templates that gives you some ideas for organization and content. For this Try It, select *Classroom site*.

Figure 4.1 Create New Site Menu

5. Name your site. The Web address Google creates for your site includes this name.

6. Click *Select a theme* and click the theme of your choice.

7. Click on *More options*. Under *Share with*, choose *Everyone in the world* or *Only people I specify*. If you want to make your site public, choose *Everyone in the world*. If you want only those you invite (students, parents, staff, etc.) to view the site, click *Only people I specify*.

8. Type in the CAPTCHA code (the squiggly letters and numbers you need to type to prove you are a real person and not a computer) and click *Create site*. Google automatically checks the availability of your site name. If it is already taken, an error message appears. If necessary, try other names until one is accepted.

9. Once your site name is accepted, your new website appears. The name of the site appears correctly, but all other areas will show placeholder information.

Figure 4.2 Google Classroom Site with Placeholder Information

Customizing the Home Page

Home is the start page of a website. It is the page visitors will see when they enter the site. The *Classroom site* template is very user-friendly and walks you through the steps needed to change features on your site such as *Homework Assignments*, *Extra Credit*, and *Contact Me*. Look for a *Tip:* link on each page for more details about customizing the page features.

Try It

Customize Student of the Month

1. From the home page of your site, click *John Doe* to open the Student of the Month page.

2. Click on the pencil icon (top-right) to edit the page.

3. Change the text in the title and body.

4. Click on the photo.

5. In the box that appears under the photo, click on the *X* to remove the photo.

6. Pull down *Insert* (top-left) and select *Image*.

7. Upload an image and click *ok*.

8. Click on the image to open a box below the image. Customize your image using the available options.

Figure 4.3 Changing an Image

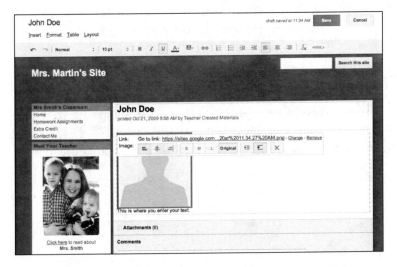

9. When you have finished customizing the page, click *Save* (top right).

10. Click the name of your site at the top of the screen to return to the home page and see the changes you made.

Figure 4.4 New Image in Home Page

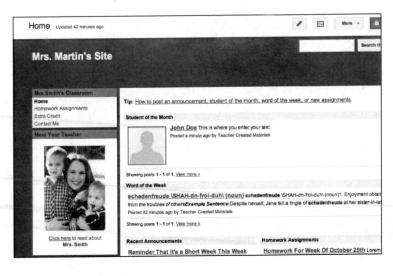

Tip The process for customizing each page is different depending on what type of page it is. Click the *Tip:* link on each page for more information.

Creating Pages

The *New page* feature allows you to add pages to your site in whatever format you feel is most appropriate. The *New page* button allows you to choose the type of page you want to add.

Figure 4.5 Create a New Page Menu

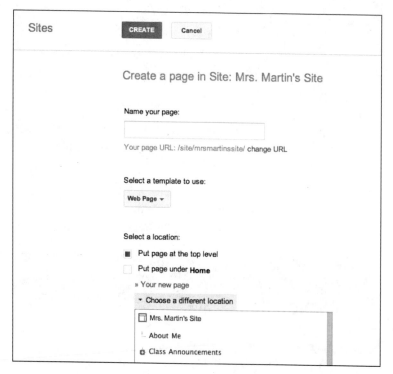

The following types of pages are available:

- **Web page:** Use this basic page to add content and features.

- **File cabinet:** Use the file cabinet to upload and share files. You can create folders for different subjects.

- **List:** Use this page to create to-do lists or assignment lists. You can easily add or remove items.

- **Announcements:** Use this tool to add up-to-date announcements to your page. While much of your content remains static, this lets you place time-stamped information anywhere on your site.

Embed gadgets on your pages as tools or just for fun. While editing a website page, click on the *Insert* pull-down menu and select *More Gadgets…*to see the Gadgets menu. Gadgets, as defined by Google, are "miniature objects made by Google users like you that offer cool and dynamic content that can be placed on any page on the Web." New, fun gadgets are being created all the time, so be sure to take a look at the Gadgets menu often.

Figure 4.6 Add a Gadget To Your Page Menu

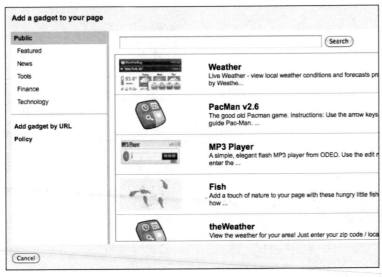

Editing Your Site

Once you have created a site, you can edit it to add or change features and content. Click the *Edit page* button (the pencil icon) to open the page editor to make changes to the fonts, page set-up, etc. The *Insert* option can be used to embed photos, videos, gadgets, and more. This is where you can bring in your *PowerPoint* presentation from yesterday's lesson, post your spelling words, or share your rubric.

Insert a Google Map in a Site

1. Open your site home page and click the pencil icon to edit the page.

2. Click in the area of the page where you would like to put the map.

3. Click the *Insert* pull-down menu and select *Map*.

Figure 4.7 Insert Menu

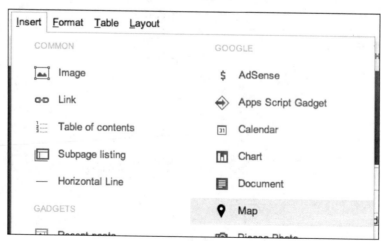

4. Adjust the map location and size to fit your needs.

Figure 4.8 Insert Google Map Window

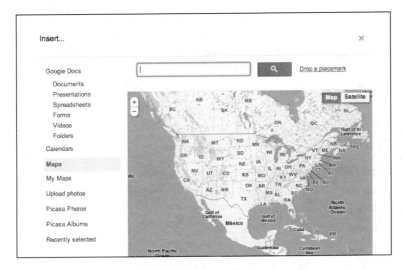

5. Click *Save* in the map window, then *Save* on the site page.

6. Return to the site home page to see the map in your site.

Figure 4.9 Google Map in Home Page

Tip When embedding *YouTube* videos, be sure to copy the URL for the video from the *YouTube* website. Google Sites can be picky when it comes to *YouTube* videos. Save the URL from your browser, not from the *share* button beneath the video on the *YouTube* site. Paste this URL in the box provided by the *Insert* menu on your site. Once you click *Save*, the video appears in your site.

Organizing Your Site

Once you have created pages, you will want to organize them so they are easy for site visitors to find. To reorganize pages, click the *More* button and select *Manage site*. Click *Pages* in the left sidebar. Click and drag pages to reorganize.

Figure 4.10 Site Page Management View

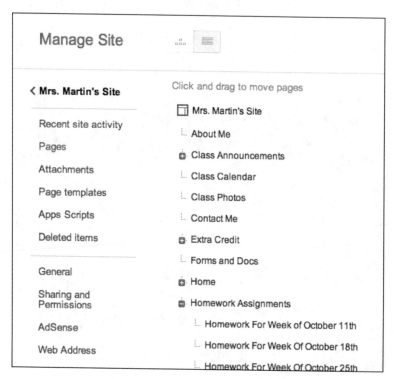

To edit the overall look of the site, pull down the *More* menu, select *Manage site*, and click *Site layout*, *Colors and Fonts*, or *Themes*. You can also access the *Site Layout* page by clicking *Edit sidebar* under the sidebar on your home page.

Figure 4.11 Site Layout Management View

Manage Site	SAVE	Preview	Cancel

‹ **Mrs. Martin's Site**

Change site layout | Configure search

Recent site activity
Pages
Attachments
Page templates
Apps Scripts
Deleted items

General
Sharing and Permissions
AdSense
Web Address

Site layout
Colors and Fonts
Themes

header
Height: 110 pixels - change logo
Alignment: Standard, Theme Default - change

sidebar:
Width: 215 pixels

Navigation: edit	delete
Text: edit	delete
Navigation: edit	delete
Text: edit	delete
Text: edit	delete
Add a sidebar item

page content
This area is reserved for site content

system footer
customize system footer links

Tip If you subscribe to page and site changes, a notification is sent to your Gmail account every time a change is made to your site. To subscribe, click on *More* and select *Subscribe to site changes*. If you are the only one editing your site, this is unnecessary. However, if you are sharing, or your students have shared with you, these emails are a very simple way to keep track of the work that is being done.

Getting Help

There is much more to sites than can be summarized in this chapter. Your site can be as simple or complex as you like. Doing a Google search for *Sites Help* or clicking on *Help* while you are working on your site can be extremely helpful. Google engineers have done a fabulous job of answering previously asked questions.

? Reflection Questions

1. How could you use a Google Site to communicate with your students and parents? What types of features would you want to include for parents? For students?

2. How could you have your students use Google Sites? (For example, could you forgo a book report or research project and have students create Google Sites instead?)

Chapter 5

Using Google in the Classroom

Google tools can be used to facilitate teacher-student collaboration, as well as student-student collaboration. In order to run a truly collaborative classroom that utilizes Google tools to their full potential, certain protocols, procedures, and expectations must be set in place. Successful learners are knowledgeable, self-determined, and strategic. They are empathetic thinkers that interact with the teacher, materials, and other learners. Effective communication and collaboration are essential to students becoming successful learners, and the more structure and direction we can give them, the quicker they will get there.

Classroom Management

Integrating technology into your classroom can be challenging. The first step to using Google tools with students is to set up efficient classroom management strategies specifically aimed at making Google an integral part of the school day.

Provide Access to Computers

Whether you have access to one computer or laptop for every student or one computer for the whole class, your students can use Google tools.

Classroom Computers

Here are some ideas on managing student use of desktop or laptop computers in the classroom.

- If you have a couple of computers to set up in the classroom, put them in the back so that the monitors face you, and you can watch what your students are doing even when you are working with other members of the class.

- Label each computer so that each is easy to identify. This is especially helpful if students are assigned to computers, or if you need to notify someone of a technical issue. When students are assigned to computers, management is smoother.

- When sharing a limited number of classroom computers, organize students into groups and assign each group a day of the week or a part of the school day to use the computers.

- When students are working on small group projects on classroom computers, divide the tasks so some students are working on the computers while others are working at their desks on another part of the project. When one group is finished using the computers, they must notify the next group that it's their turn.

Computer Lab

Here are some tips for working in a computer lab setting:

- Assign each student a computer. Students can line up in number order or computer lab order in their classrooms prior to going to the lab. If this procedure is followed before leaving the classroom, getting seated in the lab goes very quickly.

- Have a set of procedures in place to help students remember to log in to the computers, sign in to their Google accounts, and sign out of both before leaving the lab. Write these procedures on index cards, laminate them, and keep a copy at each computer.

Tip Always have students wash their hands before going to the computer lab or using classroom computers. It stops the spread of germs and keeps keyboards and touch screens clean.

Build In Technology Procedures

Put procedures in place ahead of time to handle student questions and problems related to technology use.

- Post a list of all the rules for technology use in a visible place. Include natural consequences for breaking those rules, such as losing five minutes on the computer.

- Laminate the directions for frequently used computer operations—logging into computers, accessing the Internet, sharing Google Docs, and so on—on index cards and connect them with a circle ring. Keep a set with each computer.

- Create classroom technology jobs for students to make management easier and give the students responsibility. For example, choose a student Technology Manager who knows the ins and outs of your technology management plan, in case there is a substitute teacher. This person would also make a great teacher's assistant when you are there. Nearly every class has a "whiz kid" that can act as Technical Manager, helping resolve printer and computer issues. Finally, appoint a Closure Manager, who makes sure work areas are neat and students have logged off or shut down properly before they are dismissed. Create an application form for students, as these jobs are privileges and for only the most qualified.

- Institute an "Ask three before me" policy. Tell students they must ask three peers for help before they come to the teacher. Remind them that the Technology Manager and Technical Manager are their first go-to assistants.

- When you are presenting a lesson or giving instructions, have the students turn their monitors off, close their laptops, or turn their tablets face-down so their full attention is focused on you.

- Never assume you know it all! Offer a free pencil, bathroom pass, or other reward to any student who teaches you something new.

Keeping Students Safe

Our students spend hours online. In 2010, more than 7.5 million children under the age of 13 had Facebook pages (Consumer Reports 2011). Children have 24/7 access to the world, and yet many, if not most, do not know how to behave safely online. They have no idea of the power, or the risk, they have at their fingertips.

As a result of the enactment of the Children's Internet Protection Act (CIPA: Public Law 106-554; 114 Stat. 2763A-336) in 2000, which mandates that schools implement Internet safety policies and technology protection measures to receive E-Rate funding, most schools have developed acceptable use policies and implemented filtering and other technology-based solutions to help protect children. However, according to the School and Family Education (SAFE) Internet Act of 2009 (S.1047.IS), most elementary and secondary school educators have received little or no professional development training on Internet safety. As a result, many students receive little or no education on safe, responsible, and ethical use of the Internet and other new media. Your school or district may have an Internet safety curriculum in place at this time, so look into this for rules and guidelines to share with your students. Below are some not-so-common-common-sense guidelines to share with your students prior to "letting them loose" on the Internet.

Passwords

Share these guidelines with students to help them protect their online privacy.

- Create a password that is at least eight characters in length. It is best to include one capital letter and a number in your password.

- Do not use obvious passwords such as your name, your birthday, or names of family members or pets. They are too easy to figure out.

- Do not use a sequence of letters or numbers such as *12345* or *abcde*. Over a million Facebook and MySpace users had their passwords stolen in 2010 because they used sequences like *12345* and *abc123*.

- Never share your passwords with anyone but your parents or teacher. Even best friends get in fights, so do not share your passwords with your friends.

- Keep your password in a safe place in case you forget it.

Online Safety

Although our schools have excellent filters, students find many ways to work around them. The following guidelines are geared toward kids who are online off campus, but the rules need to apply at school as well.

- Never give any personal information to anyone you meet online. That means first or last names, phone numbers, passwords, birth dates or years, or credit card information.

- Never post your location or what you plan to do. Do not share your schedule, the name of your school, or where you will have soccer practice today.

- When you receive funny emails with questionnaires, delete them. You never know how many people will receive your information through a forward. Your privacy is too valuable. Your parents won't mind if you blame them for not letting you participate.

- Delete emails, instant messages, and texts from people you don't know. If it is important, they will contact you through your parents. You cannot be sure who you are talking to.

- There is no such thing as "private" on the Internet. Anything you post can be found again, even if you think you have deleted it forever. Watch what you say and what you post. Don't post anything you wouldn't want your parents or your teachers to see.

- Do not post pictures of yourself. Even if they are cute and you want everyone to see them, beware that others can figure out your location and information about you from a photograph.

- Do not post or email pictures of other people. You may think it is hilarious, but this can be a form of cyber-bullying and it is against the law.

- Always get your parents' or teacher's permission before downloading anything. This helps to ensure that what you put on your computer is safe and virus-free.

Direct students and parents to the Safe Online Surfing Internet Safety Challenge (http://usa-sos.org/), a free interactive, educational program available to public and private schools nationwide. This competitive online program for grades 3–8 is designed to meet Federal and State Internet safety mandates, focusing on cyber safety and Internet citizenship concepts. For younger students, beginning at about age five, parents and teachers can go to NetSmartzKids (http://www.netsmartzkids.org) for interactive games, videos, and lessons on safety on and offline. This site was created by the National Center for Missing and Exploited Children, whose mission it is to provide safety information and resources to parents, teachers, law enforcement, and other professionals.

Google SafeSearch

Google SafeSearch should be set to *strict* on all student computers and locked with a password. If more than one browser is installed on a student computer (e.g., Explorer, Chrome, Safari), you will need to set SafeSearch on each browser separately. You can tell at a glance, even from across the room, that SafeSearch is locked if you see the colored balls in the upper right corner of the search screen.

Figure 5.1 Google SafeSearch Lock

Student Google Accounts

Now that you have all the procedures in place, it is time to get your students logged in to Google. The easiest way to do this is with *Google Apps for Education Edition*. Google Apps is a suite of Google applications that brings together Google tools for your classroom, school, or district. This is a hosted service that lets schools and districts use a variety of Google products, including Email, Google Docs, Google Calendar, and Google Sites, on their own domain (such as www.anyschool.com). You can use your district domain, or buy your own for about ten dollars. To sign up, do a Google search for "Google Apps for Education" and follow the instructions.

One of the benefits of Google Apps is that the administrator can assign students to individual accounts. Students will log on to their own accounts within the school or district domain. It is important to create an easy-to-remember naming system so that you have each child's username and password. For example, Username: [Last Name] [Initial]; Password: [Student number].

Once you have a domain name and sign up for Google Apps services, everyone on that domain gets a custom email address (e.g., user@anyschool.com) and access to all Google apps and tools. Many schools, especially K–8, are reluctant to set up emails for students. Google Apps for Education limits emails to within the school or district domain. This means the administrator can set up the account so that email can only be sent to those within the Google Apps for Education account. You can also turn Gmail off completely.

Google explains how a Google Account is different from a Google Apps account:

> *Although Google Apps and Google Accounts allow you to access several of the same Google products, they're different types of accounts. A Google Account is a unified sign-in system that provides access to a variety of free Google consumer products—such as Gmail, Google Groups, Google Shopping List, Picasa, Web History, iGoogle, and Google Checkout—administered by Google. Google Apps provides access to products powered by Google but administered by your organization.*

> (Google Accounts Help Page)

To qualify for Google Apps for Education Edition, you need to be an accredited, nonprofit K–12 school. Home schools, PTAs, sports clubs, and student-affiliated clubs do not qualify for the Education Edition.

Sharing Google Docs in the Classroom

Once your students have Google accounts, teach them how to share with you and with other students. Collaboration is the real educational power of Google Docs.

Share with the Teacher

When students work on a project, either individually or collaboratively using Google Docs, they should always share their document with their teacher. Once a student creates a document, he or she should be directed to invite the teacher to become a collaborator on the document. Teachers can assess student progress, as well as participation, by clicking *See revision history* in the *File* menu. A sidebar appears that details every change made to the document, the user who made each change, and the date and time each change was made. You can also turn on *Show changes* at the bottom of the *Revision history* sidebar and each student's edits and comments appear in the document in a different color, making it easy to see who is responsible for each edit. It is important for student growth and learning that you review and assess students' documents frequently and provide ongoing feedback as your students work.

Figure 5.2 Revision History

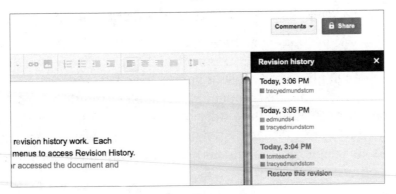

Sharing with Other Students

When students share Google Docs—be they documents, spreadsheets, or presentations—they can work together without physically being in the same space. Students working together can make changes directly to the text or comment on each other's work using the *Insert Comment* feature. Because they have shared with you, you can closely monitor students' interaction. Using Google tools to collaborate in an online environment opens up a new set of contributors. Students from different classes, different schools, anywhere in the world can work on the same document at the same time. When students are working on a project, they are notified if one of their partners is editing at the same time. Changes are made practically immediately, so it seems as though students are right next to each other.

Google Documents in the Classroom

Because Google documents can be shared, they are useful for collaborative projects. Students can work individually or in groups and the teacher can provide input and assessment throughout the project. This section provides some suggestions for types of projects students can collaborate on in Google Documents.

Introductory Activity for Google Documents

Display an illustration or photograph with lots of detail. Have students create a Google Document and begin a story based on the photograph. After a few minutes, have students share their document with another student. Each student should add to the other's story, then share the story back and forth a few times until both stories are finished. Students learn how word processing works in Google Documents and how to share their documents with others.

Publishing Google Documents to the Web

Google Docs can provide an authentic purpose and audience for students' work. Students can publish their work to the Internet for peers, parents, and others to view. Documents can be published by selecting *Publish to the Web* in the *Share* pull-down menu. When a document is set to *Public on the Web*, a URL (address) is created and students can email this to viewers who can click the link to see the published work, even without a Google account. HTML code is also provided so that the document can be embedded in a website.

Google Presentations in the Classroom

Whether it is used as a tool for teaching, or a tool for learning, Google Presentations can be utilized in any classroom. Many teachers spend hours creating *Microsoft PowerPoint*® or other slide show presentations to use as part of teacher-directed lessons. This is especially true in middle and high schools. With Google Presentations, slide shows are stored in The Cloud and are accessible from anywhere via the Internet so they can be edited at any time and shared with other educators.

Students can begin learning to build slide show presentations from the earliest grades. Instead of the usual group research report with a poster, have students create a slide show in Google Presentations to play for the class. As they do their research and build their presentation, students work together to analyze and evaluate the material they include on their slides. The collaborative nature of Google Presentations makes it a valuable addition to the classroom.

Backchannel with Google Presentations

"Backchannel" communication is when an audience actively participates during a presentation by sending short messages to the presenter that are then shared with the group. Google Presentations has backchannel communication built-in. When you present a slide show in Google Presentations, you see a little dialog cloud in the corner that says *View Together*. Clicking here opens a sidebar on the right side of the presentation screen. At the top of the sidebar is a URL to share with your audience. Viewers access the Internet on desktop or laptop computers, tablets, smart phones, or other Internet-enabled devices, type in the presentation URL, and become part of the presentation.

 I have found that in a large group, it works well to go to a URL shortening website, such as www.tinyurl.com, and paste in the URL provided by Google to get a much shorter one that is easier to type. Another option is to paste the URL into a Google document and share it with your audience. They can open the doc and click on the link to access the presentation.

Once your audience members access the URL, they can type messages into their computer that are displayed in the chat window of the presentation. Include discussion questions in your slides and students can answer in the chat window. This is a great way to get shy students, the ones who never raise their hands, to participate in class discussions. Students can post links to *Picassa®* photos or *YouTube®* videos to display or play them right in the chat window. Present a vocabulary word with a definition and ask students to post photos that represent that word.

Introductory Activity for Google Presentations

Try introducing your class to Google Presentations with a simple vocabulary lesson. Give groups of students a few vocabulary words for which to create slides. Together they can define the words, insert pictures, and even add a video. Students should then share their short presentations with the class. Another option is to create one presentation for the entire class, shared by all. Give each student a vocabulary word to research and create a slide. The entire class can then view the large, collaborative project.

Google Drawing in the Classroom

Google Drawing allows teachers and students to work together to create visual organizers and images. Google Drawing can be used on a smart board during class brainstorming and discussions to create and fill in visual organizers. Flowcharts or diagrams can be created and shared with students, and then students can fill in the text. Or, students can be given text and asked to organize it using Google Drawing. Students can collaborate to create any kind of visual organizer or infographic to include in their Google Documents and Presentations.

Here are some graphics you and your students can create in Google Drawings:

- mind maps or thinking maps

- graphic organizers

- Venn diagrams

- T-charts

- cartoons and comics

- annotated photographs

- updatable classroom seating chart

- interactive timelines

 Google Drawing templates are available in the Google Docs Template Gallery, accessible by clicking *Browse template gallery* at the top of the Google Docs home page.

Google Forms and Spreadsheets in the Classroom

Google Forms and Spreadsheets together provide a powerful tool for increasing student engagement. Google Forms allow you and your students to create a webpage that gathers input and drops it directly into a spreadsheet. From there, the data can be analyzed, played with, graphed, shared, etc. There are myriad uses for Google Forms and Spreadsheets in the school environment:

- Get to know your class by creating an interest survey. Have students fill out the form in class or in the computer lab, or assign the form as homework.

- Have students create a rating form, collect responses, and analyze data.

- Create reading logs and book reports that students can fill out online.

- Create a form to track student progress on long-term assignments. Include a link to students' work in Google Docs.

- Survey student interests: What kind of technology do they have access to outside of school? What would they like to study next in science?

- Have parents or students input their lunch count from home.

- Give students a pre-test via forms. Create a simple multiple choice quiz and look at the *Summary of Responses* to get an idea of what your students already know and where they need more instruction so you can tailor your teaching to their needs.

- Ask parents to sign up for classroom duties, volunteer for field trips, or let you know they want to share their talents for Career Day, all via forms.

Figure 5.3 Sample Google Forms

Introductory Activity for Google Forms and Spreadsheets

When you introduce students to Google Forms and Spreadsheets for the first time, it is best to start by having students fill out a simple form so that you can show them the "bells and whistles" when you share their data in a spreadsheet. Create a form that asks for students' names and favorite color or movie. When all students have filled out the form, share the spreadsheet with the class. Show them how to sort the columns and create different charts and graphs from the data. Once students have some experience with surveys, have them create their own survey, provide a link to their classmates, and then have them fill out each other's forms. As always, they should share their forms with the teacher so you can monitor responses.

Mark Bantle, a middle school industrial arts teacher, provides a one-question form to his students. It asks the question, "What is one word that describes a quality that employers look for when hiring?" The students type one word into the form and a spreadsheet is populated. Mr. Bantle then takes the results, usually an extensive list of thirty or more words, and pastes them into a *Wordle*. It makes a beautiful word cloud, appropriate for any bulletin board or display. If you have never created a Wordle, go to http://www.wordle.com. It is amazing.

Classroom Collections Management

Some simple file naming protocols can help you manage Google Docs. For single classes, a collection should be created for each student. For multiple classes, each period should have its own collection. Students should use a common naming scheme for their files, as given below.

- Secondary (multiple classes): [class period] [last name] [first name] [assignment name]. This lets you sort by document name and period for each class, by last name to find a particular student's documents, or by assignment to view all students' work on a particular assignment.

- Elementary: [last name] [first name] [assignment name]. This lets you sort by last name to see each student's body of work, or by assignment to see all students' work on a particular assignment.

Google Sites in the Classroom

Google Sites allow you to create a fairly robust website for your classroom or school in a short period of time. When students create websites of their own, they are engaged, motivated, and excited to learn and share.

For example, instead of assigning students to write a report on a state, have them build a website about that state. Once they have completed their research, students can create a Google Site for their assigned state. Begin by having them create a homepage with the name of their state, the motto, and a current event. They can choose their theme at this time, and decide how they want their Web page to appear. The teacher can provide specific topics for the research project, which may include history, resources, industry, tourism, or fun facts, and students can create a page for each topic.

 When creating their site, students should type their paragraphs in Google Docs, rather than directly on the site, so they can take advantage of the spell-checker, as Google Sites does not include one. In addition, when students want to embed photos in their sites, they can use the advanced search feature from Google to search for copyright-free images.

Figure 5.4 Student Google Site

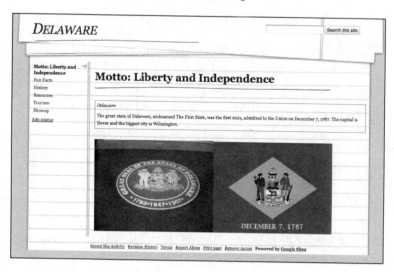

Here are some other uses for Google Sites in the classroom:

- Post homework, calendar, announcements, etc. to a class website.

- Have students create a website for a character from a novel or book.

- Set up a classroom wiki site to which students can add information.

- Provide links, post presentations, and upload documents for students who missed class or need a review.

- Post project guides so students can access them any time.

- Create online lab reports in Google Forms and embed them in your website for students to fill out.

- Add forms to your website to collect responses from students, parents, or anyone else.

Tip Share Google Sites with students and have them share their sites with you, just like Google Docs. While viewing your site's home page, pull down the *More* menu and select *Sharing and Permissions*. Select *Share this site* to view the options to invite people as viewers and editors. You can change owners here as well.

General Teacher Tips

Technology can be daunting if you are a digital immigrant. Here are some general tips to help you get started using Google tools in your classroom.

- **Don't give up.** Have you ever heard the expression, "Rome wasn't built in a day?" Well, Rome didn't have hundreds of standards to cover either. Take a deep breath and accept that the first lesson is not going to be perfect. Be flexible and adjust as you learn to use each Google tool.

- **Maintain modest goals.** Technology includes powerful learning tools, but remember that the use of technology is not the end of direct instruction as we know it. When introducing computers in your classroom, start with a small task such as a Google Images search and move on from there. Our students tend to be bigger risk-takers than we are. As you begin to feel comfortable, you can increase your repertoire of Google-based classroom activities.

- **Have a backup plan.** Backup plans, always a necessity, are even more crucial when using technology. When the Internet goes down at school, you are blessed with a teachable moment. Have an alternate plan in mind just in case.

- **Practice.** Be sure that you have "played" with the tools you plan to share with your students. You will feel more comfortable if you have some experience before you work with your students. Do not be frustrated if you can't answer every question. Just say, "Well, let's try it and see what happens." Google is a safe place to do this. You can always hit the back button or *Undo*.

- **Ask for help.** While digital natives and the TAMTAN generation surround us, many of us are digital immigrants who were not born into the digital world. Some of us still print out our emails and know what a ditto machine is. Welcome opportunities to learn from your students, and lean on those teachers that are just a bit more "techie" than you are.

? Reflection Questions

1. How will your students access computers to use Google tools?

2. What management protocols need to be developed before they begin?

3. How will you introduce the first Google tool to your class? Plan a specific activity.

4. Who is your "go to" technology person at your site? Who can you brainstorm with when you have new ideas you want to incorporate into classroom instruction?

Chapter 6

Increasing Your Productivity with Google

Search

If you picked up this book and flipped straight to this chapter, know that the information here is a variation on a theme: Google is a timesaver. Some nuts and bolts were covered in the previous pages. The purpose of this section is to provide teachers and administrators with ways Google tools can be used to make their day go a little smoother and perhaps even get them out of the office or classroom a tad earlier.

Google Forms

Google Forms is perhaps my very favorite Google tool. Forms can be your best friend when you need to gather and organize information quickly and accurately. Not a day goes by that I don't need some sort of information from somebody. With Google Forms, I can create a simple survey or questionnaire and send it to everyone for whom I have an email address. I can get feedback right away without ever lifting a phone or a pen. Here are some ways Google Forms and Spreadsheets can help you.

Parent Communication

Communication with parents is necessary and ongoing. It is important that we keep track of these conversations. There is nothing more awkward than having a parent call to follow up on a past conversation, and having to shuffle through papers in order to remember what the discussion was about. To aid in organization of communication data, create a Google Form to keep records of all your parent contacts. Each time you have a conversation with a parent, fill out the form. The information is saved in a spreadsheet so you can get to it quickly and easily.

Figure 6.1 Sample Parent Communication Form

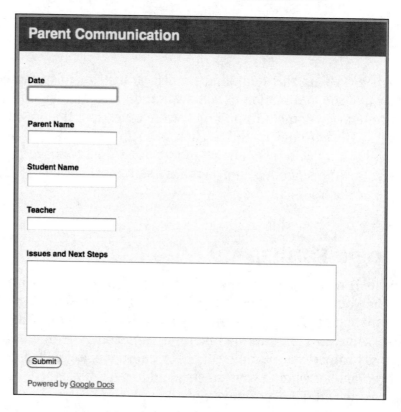

Figure 6.2 Sample Parent Communication Form Spreadsheet

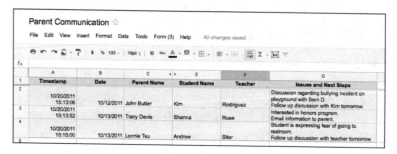

Staff Communication

As a principal, any time I have a quick question for my staff, I can create a Google Form, email it out, and have responses within hours—no more hunting people down in the teacher's lounge, littering mailboxes with memos, or interrupting class time with "a quick question." For example, during our last staff meeting, a few of us discussed our school goal for this year's standardized test. In order to get an idea of how the staff felt, I created a form, sent it out, and received results within the day. I can easily see the results by looking at the summary of responses.

Figure 6.3 Sample Staff Survey Form

Results were returned in a spreadsheet format and Google Forms automatically timestamped each response. You can click on *Form* in the spreadsheet and choose *Show summary of responses*, to get a nice, simple graph of the results.

Figure 6.4 Staff Survey Summary of Responses

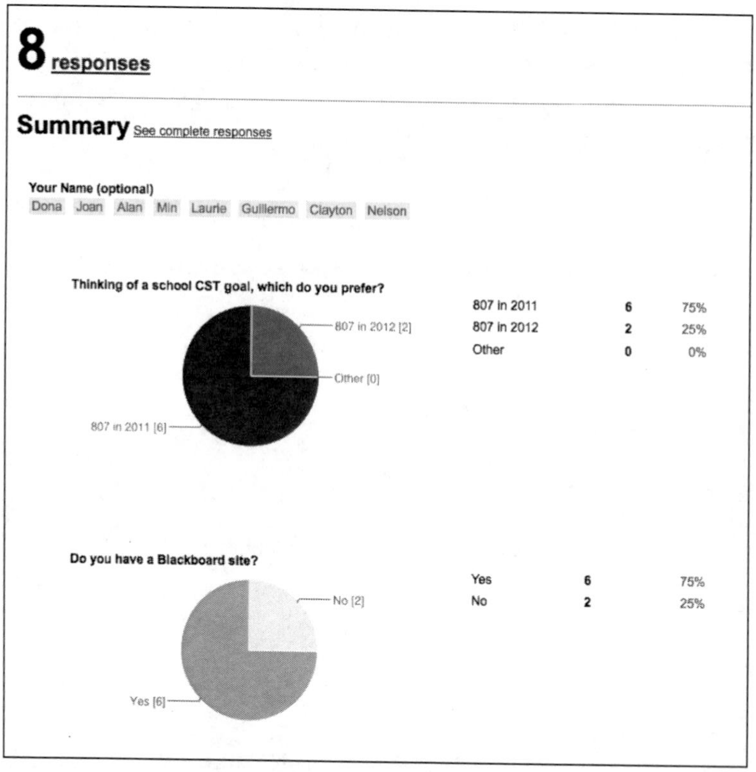

Walk-Through Observations

Many people in a district or building site conduct classroom observations, such as principals, coaches, lead/master teachers, and superintendents. Whether formal observations or informal classroom visits, Google Forms can provide a simple way to document those observations. By creating a Google form for the walk through, you can document your visit within moments and access it at any time to share with your teachers or keep track of where you have been and when. There is nothing more frustrating than visiting the same classroom at the same time every day and seeing attendance or lunch count and nothing else. A timestamp appears on the Google Form when you fill it out so you can go back and check on your visit times in the spreadsheet. In order to really get the "bang!" out of using forms for walk-throughs, it is best to bring your smart phone or other Internet-connected mobile device with you so that you can document your visit right away.

Figure 6.5 Sample Walk-Through Observation Form

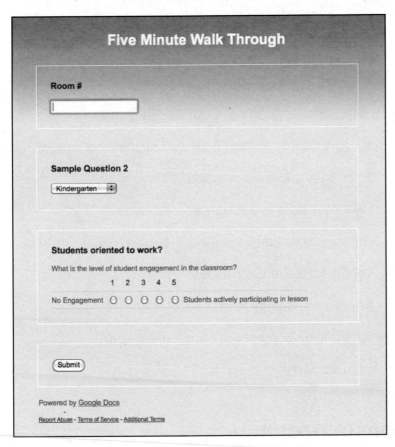

If you do not have access to the Internet as you walk through classrooms, have no fear. You can always go back to your office and fill in your form. Even though it seems like an extra step— taking a clipboard with you and then entering it in the computer when you return to your office—in the long run it saves you time and frustration. All of your data is saved to a spreadsheet for easy access later and you can throw the paper away.

 Be sure to check the Template Gallery for walk-through/observation forms. There is no need to reinvent the wheel! (See more information on Templates on the following page.)

Other Uses for Forms

Some other administrative uses for Google Forms:

- Share discipline records between teachers and administrators
- Collect volunteer information
- Take your daily lunch count
- Organize staff luncheons
- Conduct a technology survey
- Provide technology help
- Get immediate feedback after a disaster drill
- Conduct parent surveys

Google Documents

In previous sections, you have seen numerous uses for creating documents in The Cloud. The following are some additional ways teachers and administrators have used Google Documents.

- **Shared agendas:** Do you have a staff or PLC meeting planned? Share the agenda with attendees so that they may add to it.

- **IEP or Student Study Team meetings:** Take informal notes during meetings and share with parents. These can be stored indefinitely so that you can look back at any time.

- **Blue Ribbon, Distinguished School, or grant applications:** Write your application collaboratively with multiple contributors.

- **Daily bulletin and meeting minutes:** Get input from and share with staff. Save paper and copier counts!

Templates

There is not a more generous group out there than teachers. The collaborative culture of education is like no other. Google Templates allows teachers (and everyone else) to not only share what works, but to search for Docs, Presentations, Forms, etc. that works for them.

Using Templates

To access the Template Gallery, click the *Create* button on the Google Docs homepage and select *From template....* Type *Lesson Plan* into the search box and click *Search Templates* to see hundreds of templates that have been created by teachers all over the world. They can be sorted, narrowed down, and even searched by categories. Clicking *Students and Teachers* in the sidebar can narrow the search even further.

Figure 6.6 Lesson Plan Template Search

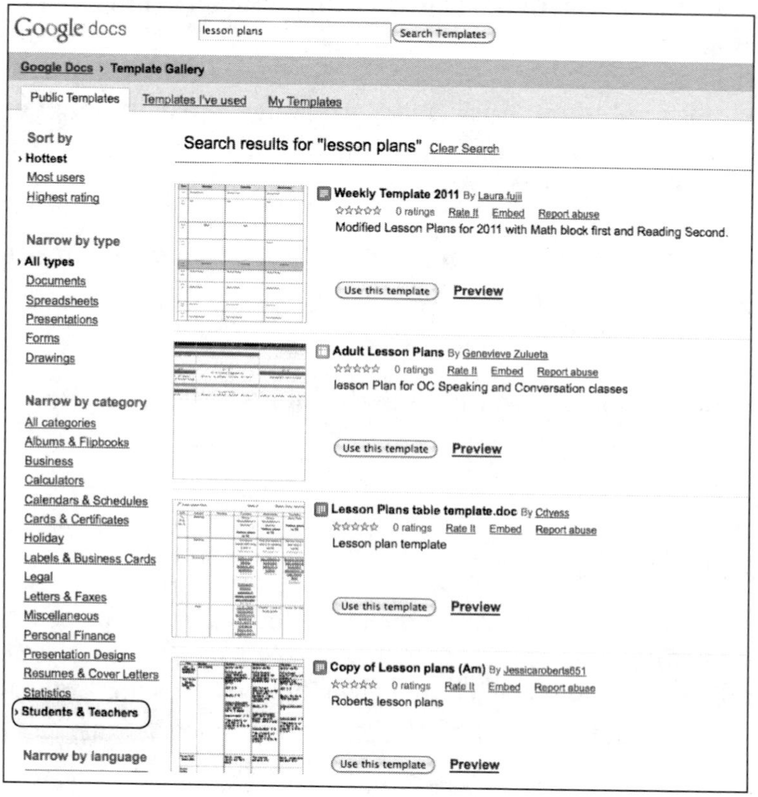

Click *Use this template* to download the template into the Google Docs folder. Once downloaded, the template may be edited and customized. The Template Gallery is an invaluable resource that can save hours of prep time.

Uploading Your Own Templates

As you create documents, presentations, and forms, they may be uploaded to Google Templates so that other teachers can use them. You should make a copy of a document before you upload it as a template so that template users will not change the original. To submit a template, check the box next to the filename, click *More*, and select *Submit to template gallery*.

Figure 6.7 Uploading to the Template Gallery

Once a template has been uploaded to the Template Gallery, move it into a folder so that it is not accessed by accident, or hide it in the Docs home page.

Google Calendar App

At nearly every professional development activity, meeting, or seminar I have attended, the question has been asked, "What more do you need?" The most frequent response from teachers is "TIME!" Studies indicate that time and its effective management is the most significant stressor category for people in helping professions, including teaching (Klas and Hawkins 1997). Unfortunately, there is no Google application that adds a few more hours to the clock. However, Google Calendar provides a smooth and simple way for teachers, administrators, students, parents, and the school community to share time-related information.

Google Calendar is a tool that can be used by administrators, teachers, and students alike. The most useful feature is, of course, "shareablity." You can create multiple calendars in your Google account. That way, you can set up separate calendars for each of your classes (or subject areas), a designated group of students, or even the entire community. Anyone who needs to view a particular calendar can see it from any Internet-connected computer, accessing it on school Web pages, *Blackboard*™ sites, etc. Google Calendar can be used to keep students and families updated about due dates, school holidays, parent-teacher conferences, assignment schedules, etc. As the calendar creator, any changes you make are automatically seen by anyone who checks. Even if you never share your calendar, it is an outstanding way for you to keep track of your own deadlines, IEP meetings, staff meetings, professional development activities, sporting events, and, of course, family obligations.

Imagine having your entire staff sharing the same calendar. Teachers can post test schedules, field trips, and computer lab schedules. Administrators may post assemblies, parent conferences, and staff meetings. Separate calendars can be created for parents, staff, and students. How nice would it be to have a shared calendar with the PTA? I always wonder when the fundraiser money is due.

Creating and Sharing Google Calendars

To create a Google Calendar, sign in to your Google account and click *Calendar* at the top of the page, or go to http://www.google.com/calendar. To create a new calendar, click the arrow next to *My calendars* and select *Create new calendar*.

Figure 6.8 Creating a Google Calendar

Then, fill in all the required information and click the *Create calendar* button at the bottom of the page. You can click the red *Create* button to add an event. Fill in all required information and click *Save*.

Figure 6.9 Creating a Google Calendar Event

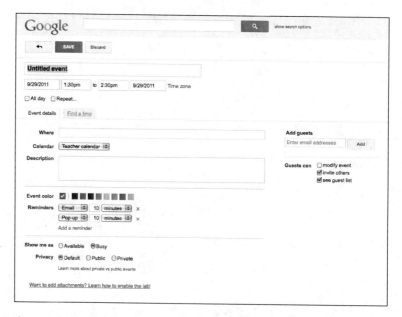

To share a calendar, select it in *My calendars*, then click the arrow to see the pull-down menu. Click on *Share this calendar* and share by entering email addresses or changing the privacy settings.

Figure 6.10 Sharing a Google Calendar

Tip You can sync your Google Calendar with your *Microsoft Outlook®* calendar. To do this, you will need to download a program from Google. Do a Google search for *Google Calendar Sync* and follow the instructions provided.

Google Groups

A Google Group™ is a user-owned group that becomes a "space" for you and anyone you invite. Within a group, you can have discussions, post documents, share links, etc. You could create a group for your grade level, department, or subject area. To create a group, select *Groups* from the Google menu bar and look for the *Create a group* button. Once you have created this group, you simply enter the emails of everyone you would like to invite. You can create a *restricted group*, where users must request consideration for group membership, or an *open group*, where the whole world can read what is going on. Most classroom Google Groups are restricted.

Figure 6.11 Creating a Group

Google groups **Create a group**

1 Set up group 2 Add members

Name your group

Create a group email address
[_____]@googlegroups.com

Group web address: http://groups.google.com/group/

Write a group description

Letters remaining: 300

☐ This group may contain adult content, nudity, or sexually explicit material. Before entering this group you will need to verify that you're 18 years of age or over.

You can opt to receive an email each time a colleague posts something to your group. You can join groups that are already in existence as well. There are currently 12,960 secondary school groups and 5,627 primary school groups. I have read about and adapted many fabulous lessons found in a Google Group for Google Certified Teachers.

Figure 6.12 Searching Groups

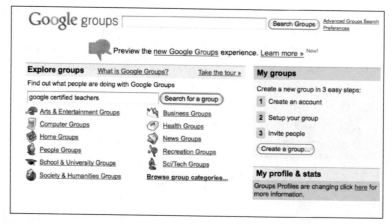

 If your school is using Google Apps for Education Edition, and you are all on the same domain, you need another Google Account in order to go outside your school domain and search through the outside groups. It is always good to have a personal Google account in addition to the one you use for school.

Going Google: Putting It All Together

Taking advantage of Google's free online tools makes sense for busy educators. Having so many communication tools in one place that work together and are available anywhere, anytime can help streamline the work process and free up time to focus on the job at hand. You probably already use a calendar of some type. Try using a Google Calendar for a while to see if it saves you time and effort. The next time you hold a staff or parent meeting, try sending out the invitation as a Google Form so that all the responses will be collected and organized automatically. Google tools are free and easy to use and they just may be for you.

Reflection Questions

1. Think about the communication methods you currently use with staff and parents. How could you use Google Forms to improve or enhance communication?

2. List three types of documents that you use regularly that you could search for in the Template Gallery.

3. What professional development topics could you search for in Google Groups?

References Cited

Association for Educational Communications and Technology. 2001. "What Is the Knowledge Base?" Accessed July 15, 2011. http://www. aect.org/standards/knowledgebase.html.

Badger, L., T. Grance, R. Patt-Corner, and J. Voas. 2011. "Cloud Computing Synopsis and Recommendations. Recommendations of the National Institute of Standards and Technnology." *NIST Special Publication* 800–146.

Barron, B. and L. Darling-Hammond. 2008. "Powerful Learning: Studies Show Deep Understanding Derives From Collaborative Methods." *Edutopia*. Accessed October 8, 2008. http://www.edutopia.org/ inquiry-project-learning-research.

Bartin, K., L. Gray, B. Gregor, L. Jackson, R. Juhant, M. Krehul, L. Sanborn, J. Timmons, and J. Wagner. 2004. "Managing Technology: Tips From the Experts." *Education World*. Accessed August 7, 2011. http://www. educationworld.com/a_tech/tech/tech116.shtml.

Bloom, B. S. 1956. *Taxonomy of Educational Objectives. Handbook 1: The Cognitive Domain*. New York: McKay.

Bohannon, J. 2011. "Searching For the Google Effect On People's Memory." *Science* 333, no. 6040: 277. Accessed July 26, 2011. http:// www.sciencemag.org/content/333/6040/277.

Bransford, J., Barron, B., Pea, P., Meltzoff, A., Kuhl, P., Bell, P., Stevens, R., Schwartz, D., Vye, N., Reeves, B., Roschelle, R., & Sabelli, N. 2006. "Foundations and Opportunities For an Interdisciplinary Science of Learning." K. Sawyer, Ed. *Cambridge Handbook of the Learning Sciences*. New York: Cambridge University Press.

Brown, E. 2011. "NIST Seeks Comments on Draft Guide to Cloud Computing." *National Institute of Standards and Technology*. Accessed July 19, 2011. http://www.nist.gov/itl/csd/20110512_cloud_guide.cfm.

Butcher, M. 2011. "Graph: How Long It Took Facebook, Twitter and Google+ To Reach 10 Million Users." *TechCrunch Europe*. Accessed August 21, 2011. http://eu.techcrunch.com/2011/07/22/graph-how-long-it-took-facebook-twitter-and-google-to-reach-10-million-users.

Cator, K. 2011. "Learning 3.0: Why Technology Belongs In Every Classroom." *Mitworld*. Accessed August 6, 2011. http://mitworld.mit.edu/video/918.

Churches, A. "Blooms Digital Taxonomy." *Educational Origami*. Accessed May 10, 2011. http://edorigami.wikispaces.com/.

"Connecting Student Learning and Technology." *Southwest Educational Development Laboratory*. Accessed August 2 2011. http://www.sedl.org/pubs/tec26/cnc.html.

Curts, E. 2011. "What Does Google+ Mean For Schools?" *Apps User Group*. August 2, 2011. http://www.appsusergroup.org/articles/what-does-googleplus-mean-for-schools.

Davidson, Hall, e-mail message to author.

Dwyer, L. 2011. "Why Google+ Is an Education Game Changer." *Good Education*. Accessed August 21, 2011. http://www.good.is/post/why-google-is-an-education-game-changer/.

Ferriter, W. M. and A. Garry. 2010. *Teaching the iGeneration: 5 Easy Ways to Introduce Essential Skills With Web 2.0 Tools*. Bloomington: Solution Tree Press.

Fijor, M. 2010. "Defining Student Engagement with Technology." *New School Technology*. Accessed August 7, 2011. http://www.newschooltechnology.org/2010/04/defining-student-engagement-with-technology/.

Google. "Our Philosophy: Ten Things We Know to Be True." http://www.google.com/about/corporate/company/tenthings.html.

Jobs, S. 2005. "Commencement Address." Stanford University (June 15, 2005). Accessed July 11, 2011. http://news.stanford.edu/news/2005/june15/jobs-061505.html.

Klas, L. and F. Hawkins. 1997. "Time Management as a Stressor for Helping Profesionals: Implications for Employment." *Journal of Employment Counseling*, 34, no. 1: 2-6. March 1997.

Marzano, R. J., D. Pickering, and J. E. Pollock. 2001. *Classroom Instruction That Works: Research-based Strategies For Increasing Student Achievement.* Alexandria, VA: Association for Supervision and Curriculum Development.

McCracken, H. 2011. "You've Got Tedium! A History of AOL in Repetitive Headlines." *Technologizer.* Accessed July 10, 2011. http://technologizer.com/2011/02/07/youve-got-tedium-a-history-of-aol-in-repetitive-headlines/.

Mo, V. July 1, 2011. *Google+ post about privacy.* Accessed August 21, 2011.

Petrie, M. 2006. "A Potted History of WordStar." *WordStar Resource Site.* Accessed 14 July 2011. http://www.wordstar.org/index.php/wordstar-history.

Prensky, M. 2001. "Digital Natives, Digital Immigrants." *On the Horizon* 9: no. 5.

Rideout, V., U.G. Foehr, D.F. Roberts. 2010. "Generation M2: Media In the Lives of 8- to 18-Year-Olds." *Kaiser Family Foundation.* Accessed August 3, 2011. http://www.kff.org/entmedia/upload/8010.pdf.

Saettler, L. P. 1990. "The Meaning of Educational Technology." In *The Evolution of American Educational Technology.* Greenwich, CT: Information Age Publishing Inc.

School and Family Education (SAFE) Internet Act of 2009, S.1047, 111th Cong., 1st session, *Congressional Record* 157, (January 25, 2011).

Schrock, K. 2011. "Bloomin' Google." *Kathy Schrock's Home Page.* Accessed August 10, 2011. http://kathyschrock.net/googleblooms/.

Sparrow, B., J. Liu, and D. Wegner. "Google Effects on Memory: Cognitive Consequences of Having Information at Our Fingertips." *Science Magazine: Science Express.* Accessed July 27, 2011. http://www.scienceexpress.org.

Staff, Edutopia. 2008. "Why Integrate Technology into the Curriculum?: The Reasons Are Many." *K-12 Education & Learning Innovations with Proven Strategies that Work.* Accessed July 14, 2011. http://www.edutopia.org/technology-integration-introduction.

Staff. 2011. "'Google Effect' Leads to Changes in Memory." *eSchoolNews*. Accessed July 27, 2011. http://www.eschoolnews.com/2011/07/21/google-effect-leads-to-changes-in-memory/.

"Summarizing and Note Taking." *Focus on Effectiveness*. 2005. Accessed July 14, 2011. http://www.netc.org/focus/strategies/summ.php.

"That Facebook Friend Might Be 10 Years Old, and Other Troubling News." *Consumer Reports Magazine*. June 2011. http://www.consumerreports.org/cro/magazine-archive/2011/june/electronics-computers/state-of-the-net/facebook-concerns/index.htm.

U.S. Congress, House. *Children's Internet Protection Act (CIPA)*, Public Law 106-554, 106th Congress. (Dec 2000).

U.S. Department of Education. 2010. *Transforming American Education: Learning Powered by Technology*. Washington DC: Office of Educational Technology.

Vance, A. 2010. "If Your Password Is 123456, Just Make It HackMe." *The New York Times*. Accessed August 14, 2011. http://www.nytimes.com/2010/01/21/technology/21password.html.

Watters, A. 2011 "Google Plus: Is This the Social Tool Schools Have Been Waiting For?" *ReadWriteWeb*. Accessed July 21, 2011. http://www.readwriteweb.com/archives/google_plus_education.php.